JN079611

小学校の 英語授業 フレーズ3000

ウィップル道子　アダム・ウィップル

明日香出版社

はじめに

　2020 年度から小学校の第 5 学年より英語が教科として扱われるようになり、お忙しい小学校の先生の中には、「英語に自信がないのに…」「英語は専門ではないのに…」などと不安を抱えておられる方が多いのではないでしょうか?

　検定教科書や副教材を活用した英語の指導方法は多くあり、急激なグローバル化による時代の移り変わりもあり、難しい取り組みに挑戦することになると思います。

　本書では、私たちが小学校や英語教室での英語指導の中から抽出した、場面に応じた「すぐに使える」「簡単に覚えられる」「できるだけ短い」フレーズを紹介します。

　私たちが試行錯誤を繰り返しながら、小学校や英語教室の英語指導の中での生徒との自然なやりとりを再現したものです。親が子に接する際のフレーズが多く含まれています。

　小学校の英語の授業でも先生方が生徒たちへの声がけに自然に使えるものを、バイリンガル子育ての中から選びました。

　小学校の英語の授業という限られた時間と空間の中で、形式的に「教科」としてきちんと英語を教えることに集中することが大切と考えがちですが、たとえ 5 分でも 10 分の短時間でも、先生が生徒たちと自然で生き生きとした英語によるコミュニケーションの時間を楽しめる「英語の時間と空間」を作り上げるお手伝いができればと思っています。

ことばの扱いはとても難しく、果てしない取り組みのように思われるかもしれませんが、ひとつひとつ、愛情を持って携わり、心が通じることで良い結果は自然とついてくると信じています。

ウィップル道子
アダム・ウィップル

音声ダウンロードについて

　Part 1 から Part 9 までのフレーズ（日本語、英語）の音声を下記 URL よりダウンロードすることができます。

https://www.asuka-g.co.jp

　小社ホームページのメニューから「本をさがす」→「ジャンル　メニュー」→「音声ダウンロード一覧」をクリックして、「音声ファイル提供書籍一覧」の中から本書を選んで、音声をダウンロードしてください。

＜トラック番号＞

　　Part 1　　Track 1 〜 37
　　Part 2　　Track 38 〜 53
　　Part 3　　Track 54 〜 88
　　Part 4　　Track 89 〜 104
　　Part 5　　Track 105 〜 116
　　Part 6　　Track 117 〜 132
　　Part 7　　Track 133 〜 146
　　Part 8　　Track 147 〜 153
　　Part 9　　Track 154 〜 164

＜収録時間＞　約 3 時間 51 分

※〈参考〉の例文、「単語を覚えましょう」「表現を覚えましょう」、および【　】の見出しは録音されていません。

※音声の再生には MP3 ファイルを再生できる機器などが必要です。機器の操作方法、音声再生ソフト等に関する技術的なご質問・お問い合わせはハードメーカーもしくはソフトメーカーにお願いいたします。

Contents

はじめに

■ Part 1 授業編

1 授業が始まる前

2 授業を始める

3 授業中

4 オンライン授業、タブレット使用

5 授業を終える

■ Part 2　アクティビティ編

■ **Part 3 学年別 英語レッスン**

1 小学校3年生のレッスン

2 小学校4年生のレッスン

3 小学校5年生のレッスン

4　小学校6年生のレッスン

■　Part 4　先生と生徒のコミュニケーション

1　先生が使う表現

2　生徒が使う表現

■　Part 5　学習指導編

1　チェックテストをする

2　テキスト・辞書・宿題について

3 テストについて説明する

■ Part 6　発展編

1 ペアワーク、グループワーク

2 発表する〔プレゼンテーションに繋げる〕

3　討論する〔ディベート〕

■ Part 7　ALT との会話

1　ALT と打ち合わせをする

2　ALT と授業をする

■ Part 8 　学校生活編

1 　学校を案内する

2 　学校生活について話す

3 　他教科について

■ Part 9 　いろいろな話題

1 　日常の話題

2 様々なトピック

カバーデザイン　大場君人

Part 1

授業編

授業が始まる前

1 生徒にあいさつする

おはよう。
Good morning.

おはよう、みんな。
Good morning, everyone.

おはよう、クラスのみんな！
Good morning, class!

こんにちは。
Good afternoon.

こんにちは、みなさん。
Hello, everyone.

やあ、みんな。〔くだけた言い方〕
Hi, there.

やあ、みんな。〔くだけた言い方〕
Hey, guys.

また会えてうれしいよ。〔休み明けなど〕
I'm glad to see you again.

また会えてうれしいよ。〔休み明けなど〕
I'm happy to see you again.

久しぶりだね。
Long time, no see.

久しぶりだね。
It's been a long time.

7月以来だね。
I haven't seen you since July.

おかえり！
Welcome back!

手を洗った？
Did you wash your hands?

消毒はした？
Did you use the hand gel?

マスクを付けてね。
Put on your mask.

イングリッシュ・ルームへようこそ！
Welcome to the English Room!

英語の授業へようこそ！
Welcome to English class!

入って。
Come in.

さぁ、入って。〔動きがある感じ〕
Come on in.

入ってね。
Please enter.

来てくれてうれしいよ。
It's nice to have you here.

来てくれてうれしいよ。
I'm glad to have you here.

3 席に誘導する

座ってね。

Please have a seat.

座ってね。

Please be seated.

座ってね。

Sit down, please.

ここが君の席だよ。

Here is your seat.

これが君の椅子だよ。

This is your chair.

床に座って。

Please sit on the floor.

床に体育座りで座って。

Please sit on the floor and hold your knees.

先生のまわりに座ってね。

Please sit around me.

近づきすぎないようにね。

Don't get too close to each other.

机の上に英語の教科書を出してね。

Put your English textbook on the desk, please.

英語のファイルを持って来て。

Bring your English file.

鉛筆と消しゴムはある？

Do you have a pencil and an eraser?

のりとハサミはある？

Do you have glue and scissors?

色鉛筆はある？

Do you have colored-pencils?

授業に必要な物はすべて揃っている？

Do you have everything for the class?

ゴールデンウィークはどうだった？

How was GoldenWeek?

週末はどうだった？

How was your weekend?

修学旅行はどうだった？

How was the school trip?

遠足はどうだった？

How was the field trip?

楽しかった？

Was it fun?

先生は台湾へ行ったよ。

I went to Taiwan.

わくわくしたよ。

It was exciting.

楽しかったよ。

It was fun.

レッスンを始めましょう！

Let's start the lesson!

さあ始めましょう。

Let's get started.

フィードバックブック〔ふりかえりシート〕を机の上に出してね。
Put your feedback book on the desk.

棚からフィードバックブックを持って来てね。
Please bring your feedback book from the bookshelf.

フィードバックブックをなくしたの？
Did you lose your feedback book?

なくさないでね。
Please keep it.

あとで職員室に来てね。
Come to the teachers' office later.

7 出席を取る Track 7

全員揃っている？
Is everyone here?

今日は誰がお休み？
Who's absent today?

今日ここに来ていない人は？
Is there anyone not here today?

出席を取るね。

I'll take attendance.

名前を呼んだら、"I'm here." と言ってね。

When I call your name, say "I'm here."
－ I'm here.

名札をつけてね。

Put on your name tag, please.

名前が見えないよ。

I can't see your name.

前につけてね。

Put it on the front.

よかった。これで見えるよ。

Good. Now I can see it.

8 生徒へ声をかける　　Track 8

散髪した？

Did you get a haircut?

似合っているね。

Nice haircut.

Tシャツかわいいね。

Your T-shirt is cute.

Tシャツかっこいいね。

Your T-shirt is cool.

Tシャツいいね。

I like your T-shirt.

Tシャツに何が描かれているの？

What's on your T-shirt?

花柄が好き？

Do you like flower patterns?

今日はうれしそうだね。

You look happy today.

あら、新しい筆箱を買ったんだね。

Oh, you got a new pencil case.

いい色だね。

Nice color.

どうして笑っているの？

Why are you laughing?

何がそんなにおもしろいの？

What's so funny?

ユキに優しくしてあげてね。

Be nice to Yuki.

ヒロにいじわるしないでね！

Don't be mean to Hiro !

9 体調をたずねる　　　　Track 9

体温は測った？

Did you check your body temperature?

みんな、元気ですか？

How are you, class?

ミホ、元気ですか？

How are you, Miho?

くしゃみをしているね。

You are sneezing.

花粉症？

Do you have hay fever?

先生は花粉症だよ。

I have hay fever.

どうしたの？

What's wrong?

疲れているね。
You look tired.

顔色が悪いよ。
You look pale.

トイレに行く？
Do you need to go to the bathroom?

保健室に行く？
Do you need to go to the nurse's office?

悲しそうだね。
You look sad.

泣いているの？
Are you crying?

どうしたの？
What happened?

痛いの？
Are you hurt?

あなたは？
How about you?

みんなは？
How's everyone?

足を骨折したの？

Did you break your leg?

腕を骨折したの？

Did you break your arm?

10 天気の話をする　　　　　　　　　　Track 10

今日の天気はどう？

How's the weather today?

晴れ。

Sunny.

雨。

Rainy.

曇り。

Cloudy.

いい天気だね？

Nice weather, isn't it?

暑くなってきたね。

It's getting hot.

寒くなってきたね。

It's getting cold.

今日は風が強いね。

It's windy today.

きれいな空を見て。

Look at the beautiful sky.

あの雲を見て。

Look at that cloud.

くじらに見えるね。

It looks like a whale.

いい風だね。

Nice breeze.

梅雨だね。

It's the rainy season.

雪が降っているね。

It's snowing.

雪だるまを作ろう。

Let's make a snowman.

東京に暴風警報が出ているね。

There is a storm warning for Tokyo.

大雨警報が出ているね。

There is a heavy rain warning.

単語を覚えましょう

●人を表すことば

私	I	私たち	we
あなた	you	あなたたち	you
彼	he	彼ら、彼女ら	they
彼女	she	人々	people

●家族

父	father	夫	husband
母	mother	妻	wife
兄、弟	brother	息子	son
姉、妹	sister	娘	daughter
両親	parents	祖父母	grandparents

Part 1

授業編

1　前回の復習をする

さっと復習をしよう。

Let's do a quick review.

前回の授業を覚えている？

Do you remember the last lesson?

前回の授業のおさらいをしよう。

Let's go over the last lesson.

前回の授業のおさらいをしよう。

Let's take a look at our previous lesson.

カードを見てね。

Look at these cards.

この単語を覚えている？

Do you remember this word?

このフレーズを覚えている？

Do you remember this phrase?

これを声に出して言える？

Could you say this out loud?

これを英語で何て言う？
How do you say this in English?

この場合は何て言う？
What do you say in this case?

小テスト〔クイズ〕をするよ。
I'm going to give you a quiz.

2 今回のテーマ・目標・活動について　　　Track 12

今日は、「色」について学ぶよ。
Today, we are going to study the "colors."

今日のテーマは「スポーツ」だよ。
Today's theme is "sports."

主なテーマは「あいさつ」だよ。
The main topic is "greetings."

今日の目標は「気持ちを表す」だよ。
Today's goal is "expressing feelings."

今日の活動に移ろう。
Let's go on to today's activity.

今日の活動の説明をするよ。
I'm going to explain today's activity.

「旅行」のことを話すよ。
We are going to talk about "trips."

3 活動について指示する　　　　　　　Track 13

ゲームをしましょう。
Let's play a game.

チャンツの練習をしましょう。
Let's practice a chant.

歌を歌いましょう。
Let's sing a song.

お話を読みましょう。
Let's read a story.

みんなで読みましょう。
Let's read together.

DVD を観ましょう。
Let's watch the DVD.

パペットで遊びましょう。
Let's play with the puppets.

ビンゴをしましょう。
Let's play BINGO.

カルタをしましょう。

Let's play *Karuta*.

「サイモンセッズ」をしましょう。

Let's play "Simon says." ＊Simon says「船長さんの命令」

「スリーヒントクイズ」をしましょう。

Let's play "Three hint quiz."

「ジェスチャーゲーム」をしましょう。

Let's play "Gesture game."

「ボードゲーム」をしましょう。

Let's play "Board game."

4 移動する   Track 14

教室へ行こう。

Let's go to the classroom.

こっちへ来て。

Please come over here.

立ってね。

Stand up, please.

座ってね。

Please sit down.

前に来て。

Please come up to the front.

後ろに下がって。

Scoot back.

ここにいて。

Stay here.

真ん中に来て。

Come to the center.

前へ移動して。

Move forward.

後ろへ移動して。

Move backward.

右へ移動して。

Move to the right.

左へ移動して。

Move to the left.

先生のほうへ近づいて。

Come close to me.

円になって。

Make a circle.

円になって座って。
Sit in a circle.

5 プリントなどを渡す、回収する　　Track 15

プリントを配るね。
I'm going to hand out some copies.

プリントだよ。
Here are some handouts.

ワークシートを配ってね。
Please pass out these worksheets.

後ろにまわして。
Please pass it back.

全部で3枚です。
There should be three handouts in total.

はい、どうぞ。
Here you are.

はい、どうぞ。〔少しくだけた言い方〕
Here you go.

1枚ずつ取って、まわしてね。
Take one and pass them on.

1枚ずつ取って、後ろへまわして。

Take one and pass them to the back.

この列は何人いるの？

How many students are there in this line?

何枚いる？

How many sheets do you need?

もっといる？

Need some more?

もらっていない人は、手を挙げて。

If you didn't get one, raise your hand.

余っていたら、先生に戻してね。

If you have some extras, return them to me.

プリントは行き届いた？

Did you get a copy?

プリントは全部行き届いたか確認して。

Make sure you have all the copies.

後ろから集めて。

Please collect them from the back.

前へまわして。

Please pass your sheets to the front.

6 時間について

時間は十分あるよ。

We have enough time.

30分あるよ。

We have 30 minutes.

5分しかないよ。

We have only 5 minutes.

残り1分。

One minute left.

あと3分あげるよ。

I'll give you 3 more minutes.

残り時間が少なくなってきたよ。

We are running out of time.

残り時間がほとんどないよ。

We have little time left.

時間だよ。

Time is up.

終わりだよ。

It's over.

皆さん、聞いて。
Listen up.

はっきりと言って。
Speak up.

もっと大きな声で言ってね。
Speak louder, please.

はっきりと言ってね。
Speak clearly, please.

聞こえないよ。
I can't hear you.

もう一度、言って。
Pardon me?

もう一度、言ってくれる？
Can you say that again?

単語を覚えましょう

●動作、行為

話す	speak	行く	go
言う	say	変える	change
書く	write	与える	give
描く	draw	終える	finish
見る	see	見つける	find
～を見る	look at	始める	start
～を聞く	listen to	遊ぶ	play
知っている	know	理解する	understand
練習する	practice	繰り返す	repeat
説明する	explain	忘れる	forget

Part 1

授業編

授業中

1 教科書を開くように言う

教科書を開いてね。

Open your textbook, please.

教科書の 10 ページを開いて。

Open your textbook to page 10.

ページをめくって。

Turn the page.

ページが間違っているよ。

You are on the wrong page.

15 ページに書いてあるよ。

You can see it on page 15.

22 ページの絵を見て。

Look at the picture on page 22.

上のほうだよ。

It's on the top part.

下のほう。

The bottom part.

右上。

The upper right-hand corner.

右下。

The lower right-hand corner.

真ん中。（※中心があるもの。はっきりしている。）

In the center.

真ん中。（※中心がないものにも使える。大体で使える。）

In the middle.

教科書を出して。

Take out your textbook.

教科書を開いて。

Open your textbook.

教科書の9ページを開いて。

Open your textbook to page 9.

2 リスニングの練習をする　　　　　Track 19

この曲を知ってる？

Do you know this song?

CD を聞きましょう。

Let's listen to the CD.

「ヘッド・ショルダーズ・ニーズ・アンド・トーズ」を聞きましょう。

Let's listen to "Head, Shoulders, knees and toes."

CDがはっきりと聞こえますか？

Can you hear the CD clearly?

3 様々な練習をする（1） Track 20

【単語を発音、発声させる】

新しい単語を見て。

Look at the new words.

誰かこれを読める人？

Can anyone read this?

先生のあとに繰り返して言ってね。

Repeat after me.

みんなで一緒に。

Everybody, together.

【キーフレーズを練習させる】

キーフレーズだよ。

These are the key phrases.

みんなで練習しましょう。
Let's practice together.

CDのあとについてリピートしてね。
Repeat after the CD.

意味はわかる？
Do you know the meaning?

【一人で練習させる】

2分間、個人練習しよう。
I'll give you 2 minutes to practice individually.

2分後に、みんなで練習だよ。
After 2 minutes, let's practice all together.

【全体で練習させる】

みんなで練習しましょう。
Let's practice together.

もう少し大きな声で言ってね。
Say it a little louder.

3回言おう。
Say it three times.

【空欄に単語を入れさせる】

空欄に正しい単語を書いて。
Fill in the blanks with the right words.

正しい単語を選んで、空欄に入れて。
Choose the right word and fill in the blanks.

【文章を書かせる】

文章を写して。
Copy the sentences.

【単語とイラストを線でつながせる】

よく聞いて、点を（線で）結んでね。
Listen carefully and connect the dots.

線を引いて。
Draw a line.

絵と単語を線で結んで。
Draw a line between the picture and the word.

5 理解度を確認する

わかった？

Did you get it?

わかる？

Do you understand?

これがわかる？

Is this clear?

もう一度、説明しようか？

Do you want me to explain one more time?

ちゃんと聞こえた？

Could you hear that well?

ちゃんと見える？

Can you see that well?

みんな見える？

Can everyone see?

先生の声、聞こえる？

Can you hear my voice well?

CD はよく聞こえている？

Can you hear the CD well?

これは見える？
Can you see this?

これについての質問はある？
Any questions about this?

6 プリントが終わったら　　　　　　　Track 23

【できた子から持って来させる】

終わったら、先生のところへ持って来て。
When you finish it, bring it to me.

出す前に、プリントに名前を書くのを忘れないで。
Don't forget to write your name on the sheet before you turn it in.

【時間が余った子にプリントを渡す】

追加の紙を配るね。
I'll give you an additional sheet.

自分のが終わったら、友だちを手伝うか、追加のシートを取りに来てね。
When you finish yours, either help your friend or get an additional sheet.

7 活動について指示する

並んでね。

Please line up.

2列になって。

Let's make two lines.

4チームに分かれましょう。

Let's make four teams.

5人のグループを作って。

Make groups of five.

1グループにつき4人ね。

Four students in each group.

ペアになって。

Make pairs.

パートナーを探して。

Find your partner.

ペアで活動して。

Work in pairs.

4人のグループで活動して。

Work in groups of four.

パートナーを代えましょう。
Let's change partners.

パートナーと向かい合って。
Face your partner.

お互いに向かい合って。
Face each other.

8 順番を決める

誰が１番目にする？
Who goes first?

誰がこれを１番目にやってみたい？
Who wants to try this first?

誰が１番？
Who's first?

誰が２番？
Who's second?

誰が３番？
Who's third?

「じゃんけん」をしよう。
Let's play 'Janken.'

「じゃんけん」をしよう、1、2、3。
Let's play 'Rock, paper, scissors', one, two, three.

話し合おう。
Let's talk about it.

君の番だよ。
Your turn.

君の番だよ。
It's your turn.

誰の番？
Who's turn?

次は誰？
Who's next?

君が「オニ」だよ。
You're "It."

〈参考〉
誰〔どれ〕にしようかな。

Eenie, meenie, miney, moe,
Catch a tiger by the toe,
If he hollers, let him go,
Eenie, meenie, miney, moe.

うるさくなってきているよ。

You are getting too loud.

おしゃべりをやめて。

Stop talking.

しーっ、静かに。

Shhh, quiet.

静かに。

Be quiet.

落ち着いて。

Settle down.

しゃべらないで。

Don't talk.

しゃべらない。

No talking.

まだしゃべっているの？

Are you still talking?

単語を覚えましょう

●序数詞

1番目	first	6番目	sixth
2番目	second	7番目	seventh
3番目	third	8番目	eighth
4番目	fourth	9番目	ninth
5番目	fifth	10番目	tenth

4 オンライン授業、タブレット使用

【Zoom を利用する】

Zoom のアプリをダウンロードしてください。
Download the Zoom app.

リンクを送ったよ。
I sent you the link.

ミーティングに参加してね。
Join the meeting.

ミーティング ID を入力して。
Enter the meeting ID.

参加ボタンをタップして。
Tap the join button.

はっきりと先生が見える？
Can you see me clearly?

はっきりと先生の声が聞こえる？
Can you hear me clearly?

見えないよ。

I can't see you.

聞こえないよ。

I can't hear you.

カメラのボタンを押してね。

Tap the camera button.

ミュートボタンを押してね。

Tap the mute button.

何か質問があったら、手のボタンをタップしてね。

If you have any questions, tap the hand button.

【絵を見ながら授業を進める】

絵を見せますね。

I'll show you some pictures.

絵が見える？

Can you see it?

2枚の絵の違いがわかる？

Can you see the difference between the two pictures?

Aの絵には、男の子が3人いるね。

In picture A, there are three boys.

Bの絵には、男の子が2人いるね。

In picture B, there are two boys.

彼らは何をしているかな？

What are they doing?

本を読んでいるね。

They are reading books.

本は何色？

What color are the books?

Aの絵では、本は赤色だね。

In picture A, the books are red.

Bの絵では、本は青色だね。

In picture B, the books are blue.

次の絵を見てね。

Look at the next pictures.

1分あげるね。

I'll give you one minute.

できるだけたくさん違いを見つけてね。

Find the differences as many as possible.

時間だよ。

Time is up.

違いを先生に発表して。

Tell me the differences.

【終了する】

今日はこれでおしまい。

That's all for today.

また次回ね。

See you next time.

退室ボタンを押してね。

Tap the leave button.

2 ネットを使って単語を調べる　　　　Track 28

【パソコンの操作について】

ノートパソコンを開いて。

Open your laptop.

パソコンを起動させて。

Turn on your computer.

画面を見て。

Look at the screen.

パソコンにログインして。

Log on to your computer.

パスワードを入力して。

Enter your password.

【調べたい単語を検索する】

今日は、インターネットで単語検索の仕方を学びます。

Today, you will learn how to search for words on the internet.

サファリを開いて。

Open safari.

空欄が見える？

Can you see the blank space?

知りたい言葉を入力して。

Let's type a word you want to know.

例えば、知りたい言葉と「英語で」を日本語で入力してね。

For example, type the word you want to know and "*Eigo de*" in Japanese.

わかりますか？

Do you understand?

質問はある？

Do you have any questions?

「英語で」を追加するのを忘れないでね。

Don't forget to add "*Eigo de.*"

オーケー。みんなうまくできているようだね。

OK. You are doing well.

エンターキーを押して。

Press the enter key.

何が見えますか？

What do you see?

英語で単語が出て来た？

Can you see the word in English?

見える人？

Who can see it?

次は、スピーカーのアイコンが見つけられるかな？

Next, can you see the speaker icon?

見つけられない人？

Who can't find it?

スピーカーのアイコンをクリックして。

Press the speaker icon.

それで発音が聞こえるよ。

Then you can hear the pronunciation.

聞こえる？

Can you hear it?

単語を調べて、その発音を聞くことができたら、合格だよ！

If you can search the word and listen to the pronunciation, you are doing great!

みんな大丈夫？

Is everyone OK?

いいですね！

Great!

【調べた単語を発表する】

では、単語を皆に発表してくれる？

Now, can you share the word?

まず、日本語で単語を言ってね。

First, say the word in Japanese.

手を挙げて。

Please raise your hand.

オーケー、はると君。

OK, Haruto.

「お菓子」という単語を調べたんだね。

You searched the word "*Okashi.*"

英語で何と言うかな？

How do you say in English?
− Sweets.

すばらしい！

Great!

新しい言葉を見つけてみよう。

Let's find a new word.

---

3 タブレットを使って授業をする　　　Track 29

【タブレットの操作について】

自分の iPad を取りに来て。

Come and get your iPad.

電源を入れてね。

Turn on the power.

みんな、大丈夫？
Are you O.K.?

アイコンをタップしてね。
Please tap the icon.

【英単語を読む練習】

今日は、英単語の読み方を学習するね。
Today, we are going to learn how to read English words.

空欄が見える？
Can you see the blank?

では、空欄に「Teacher」と書き込んでみよう。
Now, let's write "Teacher" in the blank.

空欄をタップすると、キーボードが見えるよ。
If you tap the blank, you see the keyboard.

キーボードが見える？
Can you see the keyboard?

オーケー。じゃあ、Tを見つけてタップしてごらん。
OK. Then, please find T and tap it.

次はE。
Next is E.

見つけたら、タップしてね。
If you find it, tap it.

次は A。
Next is A.

次は C。
Next is C.

次は H。
Next is H.

次は E。
Next is E.

次は R。
Next is R.

TEACHER ね。
TEACHER.

書き込んだあとに、OK をタップしてね。
After you write down, please tap OK.

そうしたら声が聞こえるよ。
Then you can hear the voice.

声のあとに続けて言ってみてね。
Please say it aloud following the voice.

すばらしい！
Excellent!

何か質問はある？
Any questions?

オーケー。次の単語を練習してみよう。
OK. Let's try the next word.

5分あげるね。
I'll give you 5 minutes.

それで、リストの上から順に単語の練習ができるよ。
So, you can practice the words from the top of the list.

準備はいい？
Are you ready?

スタート！
Start!

うまいね！
You are doing great!

じゃあ終了！
Time is up!

どうだった？
How was it?

いくつの単語を練習したかな？

How many words did you practice?

イイね。

Great.

【英文を読む、聞く】

じゃあ、次。

Let's see. Next.

空欄の下に「Sentence」っていうボタンが見えるかな？

Can you see the button says "Sentence" under the blank?

それをタップして。

Tap it.

絵本が見える？

Can you see the picture book?

今日学習した単語が入っているよ。

It has the words you've learned today.

それを声に出して読んでみよう！

Let's read it aloud!

2ページまで読んでね。

Please read it up to page 2.

読めない単語があったら、その単語をタップして。
If you have a word you can't read, tap the word.

声を聞けるよ。
You'll hear the voice.

終わった？
Did you finish it?

一番下の録音ボタンは見える？
Can you see the Record button in the bottom?

赤くて丸いボタンだよ。
It's a red circle button.

自分で読んで録音してみよう。
Let's record your reading.

終わったら、停止ボタンをタップして。
If you finish it, tap the stop button.

わかったかな？
Did you get it?

かっこよく読んでね。
Read it cool.

オーケー。始めましょう！
OK. Let's start!

みんな終わったようだね、いい？

It sounds like you all finished, right?

それでは、耳のアイコンをタップして、そしてあなたたちが読んだものを聞けますよ。

And now, tap the ear icon, then you can listen to your reading.

もし気に入らなかったら、もう1回やってみて。

If you don't like it, try one more time.

はい。じゃあ今日はここまで。

OK. That's all for today.

【タブレットの使用を終了する】

アプリを閉じて。

Close the app.

電源を切って。

Turn off the power.

iPad を前に持って来てね。

Bring the iPad to the front.

1 活動のまとめをする Track 30

「カルタ」は楽しめた？

Did you enjoy "*Karuta*"?

どのグループが一番多くカードを取れた？

Which group got the most cards?

何枚のカードを持っているか数えて。

Please count how many cards you got.

何枚カードを持っている？

How many cards do you have?

何ポイント取れた？

How many points did you get?

10 ポイントの人は？

Who got 10 points?

5 ポイントの人は？

Who got 5 points?

A グループに 10 ポイント。

Ten points for group A.

どのチームが勝ったの？

Which team won?

引き分けだね。

It's a draw.

引き分けだね。

It's a tie.

2 授業のまとめをする　　　　　　　　　　　　　Track 31

今日は「あいさつ」の勉強をしたよ。

We studied "greetings" today.

今日は「数」の練習をしたね。

We practiced "numbers" today.

今日は「かくれんぼ」をしたね。

We played "hide and seek" today.

B グループの得点が一番高かったね。

Group B got the most points.

上手にできた？

Did you do well?

ふりかえりシートを書いてね。

Fill in the feedback sheet.

アドバイスをするね。

Let me give you some advice.

復習が大事だよ。

Review is always important.

フィードバックブックをなくさないようにね。

Don't lose your feedback book.

4 終了を告げる

Track 33

終わりだよ。

Time's up.

終わりだよ。

We're done.

終わりだよ。

We're finished.

今日はこれでおしまい。

That's all for today.

どうだった？

How did you do?

どうだった？

How was it?

5 授業の終わりに　　　　　　　　　　　Track 34

活動は楽しかったかな？

Did you enjoy the activity?

授業はもうすぐ終わりだよ。

Class is almost over.

今日はこれでおしまい。

That's all for today.

今日はこれで終わりだよ。

We are done for today.

楽しかったよね？

We had a great time, right?

もうすぐお別れの時間だよ。

It's about time to say good bye.

これで授業は終わりです。

This is the end of the class.

今日の授業は楽しかった？

Did you enjoy today's lesson?

さようなら。

Good bye.

またね。

See you later.

また月曜日にね。

See you on Monday.

また来週ね。

See you next week.

また次にね。

See you next time.

週末を楽しんでね。

Have a nice weekend.

じゃあね。

Take care.

7 忘れ物がないように確認する　　　　　Track 36

イングリッシュ・ルームに忘れ物をしないようにね。

Don't leave any of your belongings in the English room.

荷物を持った？

Did you pick up everything?

これは誰の教科書かな？

Whose textbook is this?

誰の筆箱か、わかる？

Whose pencil case, do you know?

8 帰りのあいさつ　　　　　　　　　　Track 37

また次の月曜日にね。

See you next Monday.

来週会えるのを楽しみにしてるね。

I'm looking forward to seeing you next week.

良い一日を過ごしてね。

Have a great day.

良い一週間を過ごしてね。

Have a great week.

Part 2

アクティビティ編

様々なアクティビティ

【カルタ遊び】

「カルタ」をしよう。
Let's play *'karuta.'*

まず、カードを見て。
First, look at these cards.

先生のあとに繰り返して。
Repeat after me.

「カルタ」を始めましょう。
Let's start *'karuta.'*

カードを（全部）床に並べて。
Line up all the cards on the floor.

先生がカードを読んだら、そのカードを見つけて、"Here!" と言ってね。
When I call it out, find the card and say "Here!"

これが最後のカードです。
This is the last card.

何枚のカードが取れた？

How many cards did you get?

10 枚の人？

Ten?

5 枚の人？

Five?

【神経衰弱】

「神経衰弱」をしよう。

Let's play 'concentration.'

カードを切って。

Shuffle the cards.

全部のカードを下向けにランダムに並べて。

Line up all the cards face down at random.

順番が来たら、2 枚のカードをひっくり返して。

Flip two cards when your turn comes.

（カードの）名前を声を出して言ってね。

Say the name out loud.

2 枚のカードが同じだったら、持っておいて。

If the two cards are the same, you can keep them.

2枚のカードが同じじゃなかったら、元あった場所に戻して。

If the two cards are not the same, put them back where they were.

先生がやって見せるね。

I'll show you how to do it.

わかった？

Do you understand?

わかった？

Did you get it?

じゃあ、やってみよう。

Let's try.

何枚のカードが取れた？

How many cards did you get?

何枚のペアのカードが取れた？

How many pairs of cards did you get?

数えよう。

Let's count.

2 ボードゲームをする　　　　　　　　Track 39

【Snakes and Ladders】

「蛇とはしご」をしよう。
Let's play 'Snakes and Ladders.'

順番を決めて。
Decide the order.

誰が最初？
Who goes first?

誰の番？
Whose turn is it?

あなたの番？
Your turn?

誰が最後？
Who goes last?

自分のコマを「スタート」に置いて。
Put your piece on 'start.'

サイコロを振って、コマを動かして。
Roll the dice and move your piece.

3つ進んで。

Go forward three spaces.

5つ戻って。

Go back five spaces.

1回休み。

Lose a turn.

1回休み。

Miss a turn.

3 英語の歌を歌う   Track 40

ABCの歌を歌おう。

Let's sing the ABC song.

ちょっと緊張してるね。

You sound a little nervous.

緊張してる？

Are you nervous?

もう一度、曲を聞きたい？

Do you want to listen to the song one more time?

よく聞いてね。

Listen carefully.

目を閉じて、曲を聞いてごらん。

Close your eyes and listen to the song.

もう一度、歌ってみよう.

Let's sing again.

もっと大きな声で歌えるかな？

Can you sing louder?

もっと元気に歌えるよ。

You can sing more energetically.

4 DVD を観る　　　　　　　　　　　　Track 41

DVD を観よう。

Let's watch a DVD.

静かに観てね。

Watch quietly.

ちゃんと聞こえるかな？

Can you hear well?

画面がちゃんと見えるかな？

Can you see the screen well?

モニターがちゃんと見えるかな？

Can you see the monitor well?

もし見えなかったり聞こえなかったら、手を挙げてね。
If you can't see or hear, raise your hand.

ここに椅子を動かして。
Move your chair here.

少し動いてくれる？
Would you move a little bit?

【DVD に注目するように言う】（一時停止して）

スクリーンを見て。
Please look at the screen.

これは何？
What's this?

木だよね、いい？
It's a tree, right?

tree って、3 回言って。
Say tree three times.

何色かな？
What color is it?

動物を数えよう。
Let's count animals.

1、2、3、4…

One, two, three, four...

動物は何匹、見えるかな？

How many animals do you see?

鳥は見つけられる？

Can you find a bird?

家はどこかな？

Where is a house?

見つけられたら、手を挙げてね。

When you find it, raise your hand.

アクティビティ・シートはある？

Do you have an activity sheet?

アルファベットをなぞって。

Trace the alphabet.

ゆっくりなぞってね。

Trace slowly.

もし失敗したら、消して、やり直してね。

If you make a mistake, please erase it and try again.

難しいかな？

Is it difficult?

最初は難しいかもしれないけど、うまくなるよ。

Maybe it is difficult at first, but you'll do better.

もし難しかったら、ゆっくりでいいよ。

If it is difficult, take your time.

6 絵を描く Track 43

Part 2

アクティビティ編

丸を描いて。
Draw a circle.

自分の顔を描いて。
Draw your face.

友だちの顔を描いて。
Draw your friend's face.

線を引いて。
Draw a line.

好きな食べ物を描いて。
Draw your favorite food.

今日見たものを描いて。
Draw something you saw today.

ペットを描いて。
Draw your pet.

机を片づけて。
Clean up your desk.

色鉛筆がいるよ。
You need colored pencils.

のりを出して。
Take out your glue.

いちごを赤に塗って。
Color a strawberry red.

花をピンクに塗って。
Color the flower pink.

犬を茶色に塗って。
Color the dog brown.

ボールには何色を選びたい？
What color do you want to choose for the ball?

じゃあ、今度は、好きな色を選んでいいよ。
OK, this time, you can pick your favorite color.

とてもいいね。
It looks really nice.

色鉛筆を片づけよう。

It's time to put away your colored pencils.

8 ハサミを使う　　　　　　　　　　Track 45

バナナを切り抜いて。

Cut out a banana.

ハサミが必要です。

You need scissors.

ハサミを出して。

Take out your scissors.

点に沿って切って。

Cut along the dots.

まっすぐ切って。

Cut straight.

指を切らないようにね。

Don't cut your finger.

気をつけてね。

Be careful.

もし間違って切っちゃったら、先生がテープを貼ってあげるよ。

If you cut the wrong part, I can tape it.

谷折りにして。
Fold it up.

山折りにして。
Fold it down.

9 のりを使う

机の上を片づけて。
Clean up your desk.

のりが必要だよ。
You need a glue.

のりを出して。
Take out your glue.

ノートに貼って。
Please paste it on your notebook.

パーツをなくさないでね。
Don't lose your parts.

紙にのりをつけすぎないでね。
Don't put too much glue on the paper.

もし散らかしてしまったら、机の上をきれいにしないといけないね。
If you make a mess, you have to clean your desk.

濡れたタオルを取って、机の上を拭いて。

Bring your wet towel and wipe off your desk.

いろいろ作ってみよう

【オリジナルパフェ】

私はいちご、桃、リンゴとチョコレートが好き。
I like strawberries, peaches, apples and chocolate.

これが私の好きなパフェです。
This is my favorite parfait.

あなたの好きな果物は何？
What are your favorite fruits?

チョコレートは好き？
Do you like chocolate?

どうぞ。
This is for you.

【オリジナルピザ】

私はトマト、コーン、玉ねぎとチーズが好き。
I like tomatoes, corn, onions and cheese.

これが私の好きなピザです。

This is my favorite pizza.

あなたの好きな野菜は何？

What are your favorite vegetables?

チーズは好き？

Do you like cheese?

どうぞ。

This is for you.

単語を覚えましょう			
●フルーツのカード			
メロン	Melons	桃	Peaches
バナナ	Bananas	リンゴ	Apples
キウイ	Kiwi fruits	オレンジ	Oranges
いちご	Strawberries	さくらんぼ	Cherries
パイナップル	Pineapples		
●トッピングのカード			
チョコレート	Chocolate	生クリーム	Fresh cream
●野菜のカード			
トマト	Tomatoes	じゃがいも	Potatoes
玉ねぎ	Onions	きゅうり	Cucumbers
にんじん	Carrots	コーン	Corn
キャベツ	Cabbages	ピーマン	Green peppers
マッシュルーム	Mushrooms		

筆箱に何が入っている？

What do you have in your pencil case?

エンピツが 4 本。

I have four pencils.

消しゴムが 1 個。

I have an eraser.

定規が 1 本。

I have a ruler.

道具箱の中身を考えよう。

Let's make an ideal stationery box.

何を入れておきたい？

What do you want to put in it?

アクティビティ・シートだよ。

Here is your activity sheet.

ペン、ハサミとのりを入れておきたい。

I want to put in a pen, scissors and a glue stick.

ペン、ハサミとのりを自分の筆箱に入れたい。

I want to put a pen, scissors and a glue stick in my pencil case.

ホッチキス、マグネットと鉛筆削りを自分の道具箱に入れたい。

I want to put a stapler, a magnet and a pencil sharpener in my stationery box.

単語を覚えましょう

●文房具など

ペン	pen	ホッチキス	stapler
のり	glue stick	マグネット	magnet
ハサミ	scissors	マーカー	marker
ノート	notebook	カレンダー	calendar
鉛筆削り	pencil sharpener		

3 英語の授業以外の活動

外へ出よう。

Let's go outside.

サッカーをしよう。

Let's play soccer.

ドッジボールをしよう。

Let's play dodgeball.

かくれんぼをしよう。

Let's play hide and seek.

鬼ごっこをしよう。

Let's play tag.

ブランコに乗ろう。

Let's ride on a swing.

すべり台をすべろう。

Let's go down the slide.

トランプをしよう。

Let's play cards.

本を読もう。

Let's read some books.

しゃべろう。

Let's talk.

2 英語を使って体育をする　　　　　　Track 50

ドッジボールをしよう。

Let's play dodgeball.

これがドッジボールのやり方だよ。

This is how to play dodgeball.

これがコートだよ。

This is the court.

これがセンターのラインだよ。

This is the center line.

これが外のラインだよ。

This is the outer line.

これがドッジボールだよ。

This is a dodgeball.

2 チーム作ろう。

Let's make two teams.

敵のチームのプレーヤーにボールを当てて、（コートから）出そう。

Throw a ball at the players on the opposing team to get them out.

ボールが取れたら、今度は君の順番で、敵のプレーヤーを（コートから）出そう。

If you catch a ball, it's your turn to eliminate the opposing player.

ボールに当たったら、コートの外に出なければいけないよ。

When you get hit by a ball, you have to get off of the court.

敵のプレーヤーにボールを当てたら、コートに戻れるよ。

If you hit the opposing players with a ball, you can go back to the court.

敵のチームのプレーヤーを全員（コートから）出せば、自分のチームが勝ちだよ。

When you eliminate all the opposing players, your team wins.

じゃあ、やってみよう。

Let's play now.

じゃんけんぽん。

Rock, paper, scissors.

君がボールを投げて。

You throw the ball.

外に出て。

You are out.

中に入って。

You are in.

頭や顔には当てないで。

Don't hit the head or face.

3 英語を使って家庭科をする　　Track 51

パンケーキを作ろう。

Let's make pancakes.

パンケーキミックス、卵2つ、牛乳とマーガリンを使うよ。

Use pancake mix, two eggs, milk and margarine.

ボウル、泡立て器、フライ返しとフライパンが必要だよ。

We need a bowl, a whisk, a spatula and a frying pan.

ボウルに材料を入れて混ぜよう。

Let's mix them in the bowl.

泡立て器を使って、よく混ぜてね。

Use the whisk and mix them well.

コンロにフライパンを載せて。

Put the frying pan on the stove.

Part 2　アクティビティ編

フライパンにマーガリンを入れて。

Put some margarine in the frying pan.

フライパンが熱くなったら、生地を入れて。

Pour batter into the frying pan when it's hot.

数分待って、パンケーキをひっくり返して。

Wait for a few minutes and then turn over the pancake.

フライ返しを使っていいよ。

You can use the spatula.

上手にできたね。

Well done.

パンケーキをお皿に載せてね。

Put the pancake on the plate.

4 英語を使って図画工作をする　　　　　　　Track 52

貯金箱を作ろう。

Let's make a piggy bank.

紙粘土を使ってね。

Use the paper clay.

どんな形を作りたいかな？

What kind of shape do you want to make?

この見本を見てね。

Look at this sample.

先生はクマの貯金箱を作ったよ。

I made a bear bank.

まず、紙粘土をビンに被せるよ。

First, put paper clay over the bottle.

そして、自分の好きな形にしてね。

And make the shape of what you like.

もし難しすぎたら、簡単な形にしてね。

If it is too difficult, make a simple shape.

作り終わったら、乾くまで待たないといけないよ。

When you finish, we will have to wait until it gets dry.

来週、貯金箱に色をつけるね。

Next week, we will paint the piggy bank.

今日は、絵の具を使って、貯金箱に色をつけて。

Today, use your colored paints to paint your piggy bank.

色つけを楽しんでね。

Enjoy painting.

終わったら、貯金箱に名前を書いてね。

When you finish, put your name on your piggy bank.

教室と廊下の掃除をしましょう。

Let's clean the classroom and hallway.

机と椅子を片づけましょう。

Put away the desks and chairs.

教室、廊下の床を掃きましょう。

Wipe the floor in the classroom and hallway.

床の雑巾がけをしよう。

Clean the floor with wet rags.

乾いた雑巾で窓を拭こう。

Clean the windows with dry rags.

黒板の掃除をしてね。

Clean the blackboard.

ゴミ箱を外に出して。

Take the trash can outside.

掃除道具を全部片づけてね。

Put away all of the cleaning tools.

机と椅子を全部、元に戻してね。

Move back all the desks and chairs.

単語を覚えましょう

●位置を表す

〜の上に	above〔離れて上のほうに〕	〜の下に	below
〜の上に	over〔真上に〕	〜の下に	under
〜の上に	on〔接して〕	〜のそばに	by
〜の間に	between〔2つの物の間に〕		
〜の間に	among〔3つ以上の物の間に〕		

Part 3

学年別　英語レッスン

小学校3年生のレッスン

1 アルファベットで遊ぼう   Track 54

【カード】

アルファベットのカードを見て。
Look at the alphabet cards.

先生のあとに繰り返して。
Repeat after me.

A, B, C, D, E, F, G, H, I, J, K, L, M, N, O, P, Q, R, S, T, U, V, W, X, Y, Z

このカードを見て。
Look at this card.

何のアルファベットかな？
What letter is it?

【絵の中からアルファベットを探す】

この絵を見て。
Look at this picture.

～を見つけて。

Find ~.

～はどこかな？

Where is ~ ?

【アルファベット・ビンゴ】

「アルファベット・ビンゴ」をしよう。

Let's play 'Alphabet-BINGO.'

アルファベットが聞こえたら、カードに印をつけよう。

When you hear the letter, please mark it on the card.

5つ並んだら「ビンゴ」って叫んでね。

Shout "Bingo" if you get five squares in a row.

準備はいい？

Are you ready?

【名前を書こう】

自分の名前を書けるかな？

Can you write your name?

友だちの名前も書いてみて。

Write your friend's name, too.

カードを作ろう。

Let's make a card.

カードに描いてある形を使いましょう。

Use some shapes on the card.

メッセージと名前を書こう。

Write a message and your name.

好きな色を使ってカードを飾ろう。

Use your favorite color to decorate the card.

単語を覚えましょう

●カードに書く言葉

サンキューカード	Thank you
バースデーカード	Happy Birthday
ニューイヤーカード	Happy New Year
バレンタインカード	Happy Valentine's Day
クリスマスカード	Merry Christmas

●いろいろな形

円	circle	長方形	rectangle
星	star	ひし形	diamond
三角	triangle	ハート	heart
四角	square		

3 あいさつの練習   Track 56

こんにちは、僕はタカシだよ。

Hi, I'm Takashi.

日本出身だよ。

I'm from Japan.

この国旗を見て。

Look at this flag.

この旗を知ってる？

Do you know this flag?

そう、日本では、「こんにちは」って言うね。

Yes, in Japan, we say, *"Konnichiwa."*

この旗はどう？

How about this flag?

そう、アメリカでは、「Hello」と言うよ。

Yes, in America, people say, "Hello."

インターネットであいさつをもっと調べてみよう。

Check more greetings on the Internet.

〈参考〉

～では、「　　」って言うね。

In ~ , they say, "　　."

英語で 10 までの数え方を知ってる？
Do you know how to count ten in English?

1、2、3、4、5、6、7、8、9、10。
One, two, three, four, five, six, seven, eight, nine, ten.

11 から 20 までの数え方を知ってる？
Do you know how to count eleven to twenty?

11、12、13、14、15、16、17、18、19、20。
Eleven, twelve, thirteen, fourteen, fifteen, sixteen, seventeen, eighteen, nineteen, twenty.

この写真を見て。
Look at this picture.

ボールはいくつ？
How many balls?

数えよう。
Let's count.

エンピツをいくつ持っている？
How many pencils do I have?

～はいくつ？
How many ~?

それぞれの漢字は何画かな？

How many strokes in each *kanji*?

単語を覚えましょう			
●数字の言い方			
一	one	六	six
二	two	七	seven
三	three	八	eight
四	four	九	nine
五	five	十	ten

表現を覚えましょう			
●国名		「こんにちは」の言い方	
中国	China	" 你好."	（ニーハオ）
韓国	Korea	" 안녕하세요."	（アンニョンハセヨ）
アメリカ	America	"Hello."	（ハロー）
オーストラリア	Australia	"Hello."	（ハロー）
フィンランド	Finland	"Terve."	（テルヴェ）
ドイツ	Germany	"Guten Tag."	（グーテンターク）
インド	India	"नमस्ते."	（ナマステ）
ケニア	Kenya	"Jambo."	（ジャンボ）

【色】

青が好きだよ。
I like blue.

青は好き？
Do you like blue?

何色が好き？
What color do you like?

【スポーツ】

バスケが好きだよ。
I like basketball.

バスケは好き？
Do you like basketball?

どんなスポーツが好き？
What sport do you like?

【食べもの】

トマトは好きじゃないよ。

I don't like tomatoes.

トマトは好き？

Do you like tomatoes?

【好きなもの】

友だちに聞いてみて。

Ask your friends.

緑色は好き？

Do you like green?

何色が好き？

What color do you like?

野球は好き？

Do you like baseball?

どんなスポーツが好き？

What sport do you like?

単語を覚えましょう

●色

赤	red	白	white
青	blue	黒	black
緑	green	茶	brown
黄色	yellow	紫	purple
ピンク	pink	オレンジ	orange

●大小

大	big	小	small

●スポーツ

テニス	tennis	バスケ	basketball
野球	baseball	サッカー	soccer
卓球	table tennis	ドッジボール	dodgeball
水泳	swimming	バレーボール	volleyball

●野菜

トマト	tomato	ピーマン	green pepper
たまねぎ	onion	きゅうり	cucumber
ネギ	green onion	にんじん	carrot

6 体調をたずねる

元気？

How are you?

大丈夫？

Are you OK?

大丈夫？

Are you alright?

もう大丈夫？

Are you alright now?

どこが悪いの？

What's wrong?

体調は大丈夫？

Are you feeling alright?

少しは具合良くなった？

Do you feel any better?

気分は良くなってきた？

Are you feeling any better now?

具合はどう？

How do you feel?

本当に大丈夫？
Are you sure you're alright?

このカードを見て。
Look at this card.

絵が見えるかな？
Can you see the picture?

じゃあ、やってみよう！
OK, let's try!

いいね！
Good!

何か当ててごらん！
Guess what!

間違い。
Wrong answer.

もう１回、やってみて。
Do it again.

ハルカ、わかった？
Haruka, did you get it?

当たり！

Good guess!

すごい！

Awesome!

よくできたね！

Well done!

誰かジェスチャーしたい人？

Who would like to make the gesture?

8 スリーヒントクイズを作ろう
Track 61

【物】

スリーヒントクイズを作ろう。

Let's make a three hint quiz.

まず、何か選ぼう。

First, choose something.

それは何色かな？

What color is it?

種類は何？

What kind?

何のアルファベットから始まる？

What letter does it start with?

例えば、「りんご」を選びます。

For example, I choose 'apple.'

色は赤。

The color is red.

果物。

It is a fruit.

「A」から始まるよ。

It starts with 'A.'

答えは「りんご」。

The answer is 'Apple.'

では、自分のスリーヒントクイズを作ってみて。

Now, make your own three hint quiz.

友だちに聞いてみて。

Ask your friend.

黄色です。

It is yellow.

果物です。

It is fruit.

「B」から始まるよ。
It starts with 'B.'

何でしょう？
What is it?

【人、生き物】

スリーヒントクイズを作ろう。
Let's make a three hint quiz.

まず、人か生き物を選ぼう。
First, choose a person or an animal.

どこの出身？〔どこに住んでいる？〕
Where is it from?

それは何が好き？
What does it like?

何のアルファベットから始まる？
What letter does it start with?

例えば、「イチロー」を選びます。
For example, I choose 'Ichiro.'

日本出身です。
He is from Japan.

野球が好きです。

He likes baseball.

「I」から始まるよ。

It starts with 'I.'

答えは「イチロー」。

The answer is 'Ichiro.'

茶色です。

It is brown.

動物です。

It is an animal.

「D」から始まる。

It starts with 'D.'

答えは「犬」。

The answer is 'Dog.'

単語を覚えましょう			
●動物			
犬	dog	象	elephant
ネコ	cat	パンダ	panda
うさぎ	rabbit	牛	cow
きつね	fox	馬	horse
ライオン	lion	ぶた	pig

Part 3

学年別　英語レッスン

1 アルファベットで遊ぼう　　　　　Track 62

【カード】

アルファベットのカードを見て。

Look at the alphabet cards.

（先生のあとに）繰り返して。

Repeat after me.

a, b, c, d, e, f, g, h, i, j, k, l, m, n, o, p, q, r, s, t, u, v, w, x, y, z

これらを覚えている？

Do you remember these?

A, B, C, D, E, F, G, H, I, J, K, L, M, N, O, P, Q, R, S, T, U, V, W, X, Y, Z

アルファベットの（大文字と小文字の）ペアを作ろう。

Match the alphabet pairs.

【ABC Song を歌おう】

A, B, C, D, E, F, G, H, I, J, K, L, M, N, O, P,
Q, R, S, T, U, V, W, X, Y, Z.
Now I know my ABCs, next time won't you sing with me?

【絵の中から英単語を探す】

この絵を見て。
Look at this picture.

何を見つけた？
What did you find?

読めるかな？
Can you read it?

アルファベットのカードを並べて、その単語を作ってみよう。
Line up the alphabet cards to make the words.

【英単語クイズ】

アルファベットカードを使って、英単語を作ろう。
Make an English word using the alphabet cards.

そのカードを混ぜて、友だちに見せよう。

Shuffle the cards and show them to your friend.

単語を当てよう。

Guess the word.

準備はいい？

Are you ready?

【名前を書こう】

自分の名前を書けるかな？

Can you write your name?

友だちの名前も書いてみて。

Write your friend's name, too.

1 文字目は大文字ね。

The first letter is upper case.

2　いろいろな国のあいさつ　　　　　　　　Track 63

【あいさつを聞いて、出身を当てよう】

世界中のあいさつをいくつか覚えている？
Do you remember some greetings from around the world?

前に習ったことを復習しよう。
Let's review what you learnt before.

日本では、「こんにちは」って言うね。
In Japan, we say, *"Konnichiwa."*

世界地図を見て。
Look at the world map.

フィンランドでは、「テルヴェ」って言うね。
In Finland, they say, "Terve."

中国では、「ニーハオ」って言うね。
In China, they say, "你好."

ドイツでは、「グーテンターク」って言うね。
In Germany, they say, "Guten Tag."

ケニアでは、「ジャンボ」って言うね。
In Kenya, they say, "Jambo."

インドでは、「ナマステ」って言うね。

In India, they say, "नमस्ते."

韓国では、「アンニョンハセヨ」って言うね。

In Korea, they say, "안녕하세요."

アメリカやオーストラリアでは、「ハロー」って言うね。

In America or Australia, they say, "Hello."

4人のグループを作って。

Make a group of four.

まず、1人があいさつを1つ選んで、声を出して言って。

First, a person picks a greeting and says it out loud.

次に、他の人がこの人はどこの出身か当ててね。

Next, the others will guess where this person is from.

例えば、先生が「ジャンボ」と言う。

For example, I say "Jambo."

みんなは、「ケニア出身ですか?」と言って。

You say, "Are you from Kenya?"

もし答えが合っていたら、「はい」と言うね。

If the answer is correct, I say "Yes."

さぁ、やってみよう。

Now, let's try it.

3 月・曜日の言い方   Track 64

今日は何日？

What's the date today?

date は「日」のことだよ。

Date means "*Hi.*"

例えば、今日は9月18日だよ。

For example, it is September 18th.

今は何月？

What month is it?

month は「月」のことだよ。

Month means "*Tsuki.*"

September って言えるかな？

Can you say September?

January はどう？

How about January?

12 個すべての月が言えるかな？

Can you name all twelve months of the year?

すべての月を言ってみよう。

Let's try to say all the months.

「2 月」はどう言うかな？
How do you say "*Nigatsu*"?

先生のあとにリピートしてね。
Repeat after me.

1 月、2 月、3 月…
January, February, March...

今日は何曜日？
What day is it today?

月曜日だよ。
It's Monday.

1 週間の日曜日から土曜日まで言えるかな？
Can you name the days of the week from Sunday to Saturday?

日曜日から土曜日までを言ってみよう。
Let's try to say from Sunday to Saturday.

「月曜日」はどう言うかな？
How do you say "*Getsuyoubi*"?

曜日をリピートしてね。
Repeat the days of the week.

日曜日、月曜日、火曜日、水曜日…

Sunday, Monday, Tuesday, Wednesday...

いつ春が始まるか、知っている？

Do you know when spring starts?

4月生まれの人、いる？

Who was born in April?

手を挙げてね。

Raise your hand.

学年別　英語レッスン

カードを見て。
Look at these cards.

晴れ。
Sunny.

雨。
Rainy.

くもり。
Cloudy.

雪。
Snowy.

風が強い。
Windy.

先生のあとに繰り返してね。
Repeat after me.

晴れていたら、何をしたい？
When it is sunny, what would you do?

ドッジボールをしたい。
I want to play dodgeball.

サッカーをしたい。

I want to play soccer.

魚釣りに行きたい。

I want to go fishing.

外で遊びたい。

I want to play outside.

雨が降っていたら、何をしたい？

When it is rainy, what would you do?

ゲームをしたい。

I want to play video games.

ユーチューブを見たい。

I want to watch YouTube.

本を読みたい。

I want to read some books.

くもりだったら、何をしたい？

When it is cloudy, what would you do?

雪が降っていたら、何をしたい？

When it is snowy, what would you do?

雪だるまを作りたい。

I want to make a snowman.

雪合戦をしたい。

I want to have a snowball fight.

風が強いときは、何をしたい？

When it is windy, what would you do?

花火はできない。

I can't do fireworks.

5 「曜日」と「活動」 Track 66

曜日の言い方を知ってる？

Do you know how to say the day of the week?

日曜日。

Sunday.

月曜日。

Monday.

火曜日。

Tuesday.

水曜日。

Wednesday.

木曜日。

Thursday.

金曜日。
Friday.

土曜日。
Saturday.

日曜日にはたいていどんなことをしてる？
What do you usually do on Sundays?

日曜日には公園へ行きます。
I go to the park on Sundays.

サッカーをする。
I play soccer.

ピアノの練習をする。
I practice the piano.

算数の勉強をする。
I study math.

テレビを観る。
I watch TV.

お母さんを手伝う。
I help my mother.

部屋の掃除をする。
I clean my room.

記入してね。
Fill out the form.

では、みんなに発表してね。
Now, show it to the class.

日曜日には買い物に行きます。
I go shopping on Sundays.

月曜日には学校に行きます。
I go to school on Mondays.

火曜日には友だちと遊びます。
I hang out with my friends on Tuesdays.

水曜日にはスイミングスクールに行きます。
I go to swimming practice on Wednesdays.

木曜日には料理をします。
I cook on Thursdays.

金曜日には塾に行きます。
I go to cram school on Fridays.

土曜日には野球をします。
I play baseball on Saturdays.

では質問です。
Now I have a question.

ナナコさんは、金曜日に何をする？

What does Nanako do on Fridays?

6 「時間」と「一日の活動」 Track 67

この時計を見て。

Look at this clock.

何時？

What time is it?

6 時。

It's six.

7 時。

It's seven.

8 時。

It's eight.

朝の 6 時にはたいていどんなことをしてる？

What do you usually do at six in the morning?

6 時に起きます。

I wake up at six.

7 時に朝ごはんを食べます。

I eat breakfast at seven.

8時に学校へ行きます。

I go to school at eight.

昼ごろ給食を食べます。

I eat school lunch at noon.

4時に家へ帰ります。

I go home at four.

5時に宿題をします。

I do my homework at five.

7時に夕食を食べます。

I eat dinner at seven.

8時にお風呂に入ります。

I take a bath at eight.

9時に寝ます。

I go to bed at nine.

何時に寝るの？

What time do you go to bed ?

7 自分の一日を発表しよう

これが僕の一日。

This is my day.

起きる。

I wake up.

顔を洗う。

I wash my face.

歯をみがく。

I brush my teeth.

朝食を食べる。

I have breakfast.

学校へ行く。

I go to school.

家に帰る。

I go home.

宿題をする。

I do my homework.

夕食を食べる。

I have dinner.

お風呂に入る。
I take a bath.

寝る。
I go to bed.

8 学校内の好きな場所　　　　　　　Track 69

私は音楽室が好き。
I like the music room.

理由はピアノを弾くのが好きだから。
Because I like playing the piano.

学校内で好きな場所は？
What is your favorite place in school?

図書室。本が好きだから。
Library. Because I love books.

保健室。休めるから。
School nurse's room. Because I can take a rest.

職員室。先生と話せるから。
Teachers' room. Because I can talk to the teachers.

校長室。校長先生が好きだから。
Principal's office. Because I like our principal.

コンピュータ室。コンピュータが好きだから。

Computer room. Because I like computers.

図工室。絵を描くのが好きだから。

Arts and crafts room. Because I like painting.

理科室。魚が好きだから。

Science room. Because I like fish.

体育館。運動が好きだから。

Gym. Because I like sports.

運動場。外が好きだから。

Playground. Because I like outside.

教室。自分の教室が好きだから。

Classroom. Because I like my classroom.

小学校 5 年生のレッスン

1 自己紹介と自己紹介ゲーム

【ペアワーク】

やあ。僕はヒロシだよ。
Hi. I'm Hiroshi.

ネコが好きだよ。
I like cats.

2 匹のネコを飼ってるよ。
I have two cats.

土曜日にはテニスをするよ。
I play tennis on Saturdays.

玉ねぎが嫌いだよ。
I don't like onions.

君は？
How about you?

僕はユウジだよ。
I'm Yuji.

音楽が好きだよ。

I like music.

ネコを飼っているよ。

I have a cat.

日曜日にテニスをするよ。

I play tennis on Sundays.

【お互いの情報を確認する】

キミはユウジだね。

You are Yuji.

ネコが好きなんだね。

You like cats.

ネコを 2 匹飼っているんだね。

You have two cats.

土曜日にテニスをするんだね。

You play tennis on Saturdays.

玉ねぎが嫌いだね。

You don't like onions.

合ってる？

Right?

合ってるよ！
Yes!

君はアキだね。
You are Aki.

英語が好きだね。
You like English.

犬を飼っているんだね。
You have a dog.

土曜日にはピアノを弾くんだね。
You play the piano on Saturdays.

違うよ。日曜日にピアノを弾くよ。〔訂正するとき〕
No. I play the piano on Sundays.

わかった。日曜日にピアノを弾くんだね。
OK. You play the piano on Sundays.

合ってる？
Right?

合ってるよ！
Yes!

【別のペアと合流し、お互いを紹介しあう】

やぁ。
Hi.

こちらはコウジくんだよ。
This is Kouji.

ネコが好きだよ。
He likes cats.

2 匹のネコを飼っているよ。
He has two cats.

土曜日にはテニスをするよ。
He plays tennis on Saturdays.

玉ねぎが嫌いだよ。
He doesn't like onions.

こちらはミキちゃんだよ。
This is Miki.

プログラミングが好きだよ。
She likes programming.

コンピューターを持っているよ。
She has a computer.

日曜日にはゲームをするよ。

She plays games on Sundays.

はじめまして、ミキちゃん。

Nice to meet you, Miki.

2 1年間の行事、誕生日 Track 71

君の誕生日はいつ？

When is your birthday?

その月はどんな月？

What is the month like?

僕の誕生日は1月10日だよ。

My birthday is January 10th.

冬だよ。

It's in winter.

寒いよ。

It's cold.

だいたい2週間の冬休みがあるよ。

We have about a two-week winter break.

1月1日に新年を祝います。

We celebrate New Year's on January 1st.

家族と神社に初詣に参って、新年の願い事をするよ。

I go to a *Jinjya* 〔a Shinto shrine〕 to make a new year's wish with my family.

おせちは特別な食べ物で、おもちも食べるよ。

We also eat *Osechi*; special food and rice cakes.

祖父母と親戚からもらえるお年玉（お金）が大好きだよ。

I love *Otoshidama*; money from grandparents and relatives.

新しいゲームや服を買ったり、貯金したりするよ。

I can get new games, clothes or save it.

誕生日には自転車がほしいよ。

I want a bike for my birthday.

僕の誕生日は 2 月 4 日だよ。

My birthday is February 4th.

冬だよ。

It's in winter.

ときどき雪が降るよ。

It sometimes snows.

2 月 14 日はバレンタインデーだよ。

February 14th is Valentine's Day.

友だちとチョコレートやキャンディを交換するよ。

We exchange chocolates or candies with our friends.

でも今年は交換しなかったよ。

But I didn't do it this year.

お母さんがクッキーをくれたよ。

My mother gave me some cookies.

誕生日プレゼントは犬がいいな。

I want a dog for my birthday.

僕の誕生日は３月９日だよ。

My birthday is March 9th.

ひな祭りは３月３日だよ。

Dolls Festival is March 3rd.

３月は日本では学年の最後の月だよ。

March is the last month of a school year in Japan.

卒業式は大きな行事だよ。

The graduation ceremony is a big event.

「３月９日」は人気のある歌だよ。

'March 9th' is a popular song.

僕の誕生日だよ。

It's my birthday.

誕生日には iPad がほしいよ。

I want an iPad for my birthday.

僕の誕生日は 4 月 12 日だよ。

My birthday is April 12th.

春だよ。

It's spring.

暖かくなる季節だよ。

It gets warm.

新しい学年が 4 月に始まるよ。

Our new school year starts in April.

桜がきれいだよ。

Cherry blossoms are beautiful.

他にもきれいな花をたくさん見ることができるよ。

We can see many beautiful flowers, too.

入学式は大きな行事だよ。

The entrance ceremony is a big event.

新 1 年生が小学校に来るよ。

New 1st graders come to our elementary school.

１年生は小さくて、大きな「ランドセル」という学校のカバンを持っているよ。

They are small and have big schoolbags; '*Randoseru.*'

１年生はかわいい。

They are cute.

僕は誕生日に妹がほしいよ。

I want a younger sister for my birthday.

僕の誕生日は５月17日だよ。

My birthday is May 17th.

５月５日は子どもの日だよ。

May 5th is Children's Day.

かしわ餅がとても好きだよ。

I like *Kashiwa-mochi* very much.

かしわ餅を５個食べたよ。

I ate five *Kashiwa-mochi*.

ゴールデンウィークが好きだよ。

I like Golden Week.

学校に行かなくてもいいし、家族と USJ に行く予定だから。

I don't have to go to school and I will go to USJ with my family.

誕生日にはミニオンのぬいぐるみがほしいよ。

I want a stuffed Minion for my birthday.

僕の誕生日は 6 月 21 日だよ。

My birthday is June 21st.

梅雨の季節だよ。

It's the rainy season.

たくさん雨が降るよ。

We have a lot of rain.

カエルが好きだよ。

I like frogs.

誕生日に新しい傘と長靴がほしいよ。

I want a new umbrella and a boot for my birthday.

僕の誕生日は 7 月 7 日だよ。

My birthday is July 7th.

七夕だよ。

It's a star festival.

「短冊」という紙に願いごとを書いて、笹の木につるすよ。

We write a wish on '*tanzaku*'; a piece of paper and hang on a bamboo tree.

願いごとがかなうといいな。

I wish my dream comes true.

僕の誕生日は 8 月 25 日だよ。

My birthday is August 25th.

夏だよ。

It's summer.

夏休みがあるよ。

We have a summer holiday.

だいたい 40 日間だよ。

It is about forty days.

夏休みが大好きだよ！

I love summer holiday!

学校に行かなくていいんだ。

I don't have to go to school.

宿題は好きじゃないけど。

I don't like homework.

家でのんびりできる。

I can relax at home.

お盆の間はいとこの家と祖父母の家に行く予定だよ。

**I will go to my cousin's house and my grandparents'
during *Obon*.**

誕生日には新しいビーチボートがほしいよ。

I want a new beach boat for my birthday.

僕の誕生日は 9 月 21 日だよ。

My birthday is September 21st.

秋だよ。

It's fall.

運動会があるよ。

We have sports day.

運動会はあまり好きじゃないけど。

I don't like sports day very much.

「綱引き」と「玉入れ」は好きだよ。

**I like '*Tsunahiki*'〔tug-of-war〕 and '*Tamaire*'〔ball-toss
games〕.**

家族と一緒にお弁当を食べるのも好きだよ。

I like eating lunch with my family, too.

祖父母と両親が運動会に来てくれるよ。

My grandparents and parents come to sports day.

誕生日にはお寿司を食べたいよ。

I want to eat *sushi* for my birthday.

僕の誕生日は10月2日だよ。

My birthday is October 2nd.

秋だよ。

It's fall.

ハロウィンが好きだよ。

I love Halloween.

お菓子がたくさんもらえるから。

Because I can get a lot of candies.

ハロウィンの衣装を着るのも好きだよ。

I like wearing a Halloween costume, too.

楽しいよ。

It is fun.

今年はミニオンの仮装をしたいよ。

I want to wear a Minion Costume this year.

「秋祭り」にも出るよ。

I'll join '*Akimatsuri*' 〔Fall Festival〕, too.

毎晩、太鼓の練習をしているよ。

I practice *Taiko* every night.

太鼓を叩くときに日本の伝統的な歌も歌うよ。

I sing a traditional Japanese song when I play *Taiko*.

誕生日にはお金がほしいよ。

I want money for my birthday.

僕の誕生日は 11 月 22 日だよ。

My birthday is November 22nd.

秋の終わりだよ。

It's the end of fall.

11 月 15 日は「七五三」だよ。

November 15th is '*Shichi-Go-San*' 〔The Seven-Five-Three festival〕.

弟は 5 才だよ。

My brother is five years old.

だから弟は日本の着物を着て神社に行くよ。

So he will wear Japanese *kimono* and go to a shrine.

両親が写真を撮るよ。

My parents will take pictures.

「千歳飴」という長い棒状の飴を食べるよ。

We eat '*Chitoseame*'; a long stick candy.

誕生日にほしい物はまだわからないよ。

I don't know what I want for my birthday.

僕の誕生日は 12 月 10 日だよ。

My birthday is December 10th.

冬だよ。

It's winter.

寒いけど、この月は楽しいことがたくさんあるよ。

It's cold, but we have many things to enjoy this month.

12 月 25 日はクリスマスだよ。

December 25th is Christmas.

クリスマースケーキを食べたり、プレゼントをもらったりするよ。

I enjoy eating Christmas cake and getting a present.

今年のクリスマス（プレゼント）にゲームがほしいな。

I want games for Christmas this year.

誕生日プレゼントももらえるよ。

I will get a birthday present, too.

雪が降ったらうれしいな。

I'll be happy if it snows.

3 曜日、時間割り   Track 72

月曜日には算数、国語、英語と体育があるよ。

I have math, Japanese, English and P.E. on Monday.

火曜日には国語、算数、音楽と図工があるよ。

I have Japanese, math, music and arts and crafts on Tuesday.

水曜日には理科、社会科、家庭科と英語があるよ。

I have science, social studies, home economics and English on Wednesday.

木曜日には算数、体育と書写があるよ。

I have math, P.E and calligraphy on Thursday.

金曜日には英語、音楽と道徳があるよ。

I have English, music and moral education on Friday.

単語を覚えましょう			
●教科			
英語	English	社会	social studies
国語	Japanese	図工	arts and crafts
算数	math	家庭科	home economics
理科	science	道徳	moral education
音楽	music	習字〔書写〕	calligraphy
体育	P.E. (Physical Education)		

あなたはたいてい何時に起きる？
What time do you usually get up?

僕はいつも6時に起きるよ。
I always get up at six.

僕はたいてい6時半に起きるよ。
I usually get up at six-thirty.

僕は絶対5時には起きないよ。
I never get up at five.

僕は7時ごろ起きるよ。
I get up around seven.

僕は7時に朝食を食べるよ。
I eat breakfast at seven.

僕は7時55分に学校に着くよ。
I get to school at seven fifty-five.

僕は12時20分に給食を食べるよ。
I eat school lunch at twelve twenty.

一日中、学校で過ごす。
I spend all day at school.

放課後はサッカーの練習に行くよ。

I go to soccer practice after school.

僕は4時半に家に着くよ。

I get home at four thirty.

僕はたいてい6時ごろに宿題をするよ。

I usually do my homework around six.

6時半にお風呂に入るよ。

I take a bath at six thirty.

7時にテレビを観るよ。

I watch TV at seven.

僕は7時ごろ夕食を食べるよ。

I eat dinner around seven.

僕はたいてい9時半に寝るよ。

I usually go to bed at nine thirty.

単語を覚えましょう

●頻度の言い方

いつも	（100%）	always
たいてい	（80%）	usually
ときどき	（50%）	sometimes
絶対〜ない	（0%）	never

●時間の言い方

7時に	at seven
6時ごろに	around six

単語を覚えましょう

●行為、動作

皿洗いをする	wash / do the dishes
新聞を取る	get the newspaper
部屋の掃除をする	clean one's room
サッカーの練習に行く	go to soccer practice
ピアノの練習に行く	go to piano practice
ダンスの練習に行く	go to dance practice
水泳教室に行く	go to swimming school
友だちの家へ行く	go to my friend's house
祖父母の家へ行く	go to grandparents' house
〜と一緒に買物に行く	go shopping with 〜
クリニック〔病院〕に行く	go to clinic

5 いろいろできること

僕は上手に歌えるよ。

I can sing well.

君は？

How about you?

僕は速く泳げるよ。

I can swim fast.

僕は 800 メートル泳げるよ。

I can swim 800 meters.

僕は英語を話せるよ。

I can speak English.

僕は韓国語を話せるよ。

I can speak Korean.

あなたは料理が上手にできるよね。

You can cook well.

君はピアノを上手に弾けるよね。

You can play the piano.

英語の歌を歌える？

Can you sing an English song?

速く走れる？

Can you run fast?

サッカーはできる？

Can you play soccer?

野球はできる？

Can you play baseball?

ゲームはできる？

Can you play video games?

縦笛を吹ける？

Can you play the recorder?

一輪車に乗れる？

Can you ride a unicycle?

料理はできる？

Can you cook?

コウスケ君は絵がうまく描けるよ。

Kosuke can draw very well.

タケシ君はギターが弾けるよ。

Takeshi can play the guitar.

ミホちゃんはテニスができるよ。

Miho can play tennis.

鳥は飛べるよ。

Birds can fly.

魚は泳げるよ。

Fish can swim.

カエルは跳べるよ。

Frogs can jump.

オオサカ・ナオミ選手は何ができる？

What can Naomi Osaka do?

テニスができる。

She can play tennis.

オオタニ・ショウヘイ選手は何ができる？

What can Shohei Otani do?

野球ができる。

He can play baseball.

ホンダ・ケイスケ選手は何ができる？

What can Keisuke Honda do?

サッカーができる。

He can play soccer.

緑色のカバンはどこ？

Where is the green bag?

机の下だよ。

It's under the desk.

地図はどこ？

Where is the map?

壁に貼ってあるよ。

It's on the wall.

ペンはどこ？

Where are the pens?

引き出しの中だよ。

They are in the drawer.

のりはどこ？

Where is the glue stick?

箱の中だよ。

It's in the box.

ケン玉はどこ？

Where is _kendama_?

机の上だよ。

It's on the desk.

バットはどこ？

Where is the bat?

ベッドの下だよ。

It's under the bed.

帽子はどこ？

Where is the cap?

ベッドの横だよ。

It's by the bed.

地図を見て。
Look at the map.

図書館はどこ？
Where is the library?

図書館を探しているよ。
I'm looking for the library.

君はここにいるよ。
You are here.

2ブロック、まっすぐに行って。
Go straight for two blocks.

左に曲がって、まっすぐ行って。
Turn left and go straight.

スーパーマーケットの隣だよ。
It's next to the supermarket.

何が見えるかな？
What can you find?

まっすぐ行って。
Go straight.

最初の角を左に曲がって。

Turn left at the first corner.

少しだけまっすぐ行って。

Go straight for just a little bit.

右側にあるよ。

You can see it on your right.

池のそばにいるよ。

It's by the pond.

単語を覚えましょう

●場所、目印など

角	corner	交差点	crossroad
看板	sign	歩道橋	footbridge
階段	stairs	地下道	underpass
信号	traffic light	横断歩道	pedestrian crossing
Y字路	fork in the road		

何が食べたい？

What would you like?

ケーキが食べたいよ。

I want to eat cake.

（ケーキは）いくら？

How much is it?

500 円だよ。

It's five hundred yen.

ピザを食べたいよ。

I want to eat pizza.

ピザはいくら？

How much is a piece of pizza?

400 円だよ。

It's four hundred yen.

1000 円持っているよ。

I have one thousand yen.

何が買えるかな？

What can I buy?

フライドチキンは350円だよ。

Fried chicken is three hundred and fifty yen.

餃子は200円だよ。

***Gyoza* is two hundred yen.**

カレーライスは500円だよ。

Curry and rice is five hundred yen.

ミネラルウォーターは100円だよ。

Mineral water is one hundred yen.

カレーライス、フライドチキンとミネラルウォーターを買うよ。

I'll buy curry and rice, fried chicken and mineral water.

いくら?

How much?

950円だよ。

It's nine hundred and fifty yen.

どうぞ。

Here you are.

ありがとう。

Thank you.

おいしい。

It's delicious.

おいしい。
It's yummy.

甘いね。
It's sweet.

健康的だね。
It's healthy.

9 あこがれの人〔ヒーロー〕について　　Track 78

君のヒーローは誰？
Who is your hero?

オオタニ・ショウヘイ選手が僕のヒーローだよ。
Shohei Otani is my hero.

プロの野球選手だよ。
He is a professional baseball player.

投げるのも打つのもできるよ。
He can pitch and hit.

かっこいいよ！
He is cool!

オオサカ・ナオミ選手が僕のヒーローだよ。
Naomi Osaka is my hero.

プロのテニス選手だよ。

She is a professional tennis player.

全米オープン女子シングルスの1位だよ。

She is the US Open Women's Singles champion.

すばらしいね！

She is fantastic!

Hikakin が僕のヒーローだよ。

Hikakin is my hero.

彼は有名なユーチューバーだよ。

He is a famous YouTube personality.

彼は音楽も得意だよ。

He is good at music, too.

彼はおもしろくて優しいよ。

He is funny and kind.

僕もいつかユーチューバーになりたいよ。

I want to be a YouTube personality someday.

僕は科学者になりたいので、理科の勉強をがんばっているよ。

I want to be a scientist, so I'm studying science hard.

僕は芸術家になりたいので、図工の勉強をがんばっているよ。

I want to be an artist, so I'm studying arts and crafts hard.

僕は作家になりたいので、国語の勉強をがんばっているよ。

I want to be a writer, so I'm studying Japanese hard.

僕は歌手になりたいので、音楽の勉強をがんばっているよ。

I want to be a singer, so I'm studying music hard.

僕はスポーツ選手になりたいので、体育の勉強をがんばっているよ。

I want to be an athlete, so I'm studying P.E. hard.

僕はまだ決めていないから、のんびりしているよ。

I haven't decided yet, so I'm relaxed.

単語を覚えましょう

●芸術、音楽など

芸術	art	芸術家	artist
音楽	music	音楽家	musician
歌	song	歌手	singer
ピアノ	piano	ピアニスト	pianist
バイオリン	violin	バイオリニスト	violinist
ギター	guitar	ギタリスト	guitarist

小学校 6 年生のレッスン

1 自己紹介と「Guess Who?」クイズ　　Track 80

【自己紹介】

自己紹介の練習をしましょう。
Let's practice self-introduction.

自己紹介をするよ。
Let me introduce myself.

自己紹介の仕方だよ。
This is how you introduce (yourself).

聞いてね。
Listen to me.

私の名前は山田リサです。
My name is Risa Yamada.

名前を英語で言うときは、名前そして姓を言うんだ。
When you say your name in English, say your first name and then your family name.

京都出身だよ。
I am from Kyoto.

自分のことを話すときは「I」から話すといいよね。
When you talk about yourself, say "I."

「I am from ~」で「〜出身です」って意味だよ。
"I am from ~" means "~ *syusshin desu*."

「I am ~」と言うときは、自分のことを話すよ。
When you say "I am ~", you are talking about yourself.

例えば、「料理が得意だよ」とか。
For example, "I am good at cooking."

そして、好きなものとか話すといいよね。
And, you can talk about your favorite things.

「I like ~」で「私は〜が好きです」という意味だよ。
"I like ~" means "*Watashi wa ~ ga sukidesu*."

すしが好きだよ。
I like *sushi*.

誕生日は７月９日だよ。
My birthday is on July 9th.

誕生日を言うときは、まず月、そして日にちを言うんだったね。

When you say your birthday, you first say the month and then the date.

自己紹介をした後、友だちからいくつか質問を受けてもいいよ。

After you introduce yourself, allow your friends to ask you questions as well.

「何か質問はある？」と言うんだ。

You can say "Do you have any questions?"

そして、みんなも質問してね。

And others can ask questions as well.

「Do you ~?」と言うよ。

You can say "Do you ~?"

「何が好きですか」は「What things do you like?」だよ。

"*Nani ga suki desuka*" is "What things do you like?"

じゃあ、何か質問はある？

Well, do you have any questions?

はい。

Yes.

どんなスポーツが好きですか？

What sports do you like?

サッカーが好きです。

I like soccer.

オーケー。じゃあ、みんなの番だよ。

OK. It's your turn.

【まとめる】（友だちに伝える）

誰かもう1回、友だちを紹介してもらえますか？

Can anyone reintroduce your friend, please?

reintroduce とは「もう1回紹介する」って意味ね。

Reintroduce means "*mouikkai syoukai suru.*"

誰か私のことをクラスのみんなにもう1回紹介してくれる？

Will someone reintroduce me to the class?

こういうときは、「She」から話すといいよね。

In this case, use "She."

彼女は山田リサです。

She is Risa Yamada.

京都に住んでいるよ。

She lives in Kyoto.

「She lives」って言えるかな？

Can you say "She lives"?

すしが好きだよ。
She likes *sushi*.

料理が得意だよ。
She is good at cooking.

誕生日は7月9日だよ。
Her birthday is on July 9th.

サッカーが好きだよ。
She likes soccer.

何か質問はありますか？
Do you have any questions?

【"Guess Who?" クイズ】

「誰でしょう？」ゲームをしよう。
Let's play "Guess Who?"

こういうルールだよ。
This is the rule.

質問をして、誰か当ててね。
Ask a question and guess who the person is.

例えば、男子か女子か？
For example, is it a boy or a girl?

女子だよ。

It is a girl.

アイスクリームは好き？

Does she like ice cream?

いいえ、好きじゃないよ。

No, she doesn't.

すしが好き？

Does she like *sushi*?

うん、好きだよ。

Yes, she does.

どこに住んでいる？〔どこの出身？〕

Where is she from?

京都出身だよ。

She is from Kyoto.

誰かわかった人は、手を挙げてね。

When you can guess who it is, raise your hand.

それは山田先生？

Is it Ms.Yamada?

正解！

Yes!

私たちの国（の紹介）について話しましょう。

Let's talk about our country.

日本にはたくさんのおもしろい場所があるよ。

We have many interesting places in Japan.

日本にはたくさんの伝統的な建物があるよ。

We have many traditional buildings in Japan.

「日本」で始めることもできるんだ。

You can also start with "Japan."

日本にはたくさんの人気の店があるよ。

Japan has many popular stores.

日本にはたくさんのおいしいレストランがあるよ。

Japan has many delicious restaurants.

日本にはたくさんのおいしい食べ物があるよ。

We have many delicious foods in Japan.

有名な何かを紹介するのもいい考えだよね。

It is a good idea to introduce something famous.

話すのに「famous for」を使って、例えば、

Use "famous for" to talk about, for example,

北海道は「雪まつり」で有名だよ。

Hokkaido is famous for "The Snow Festival."

それがどんなものかを説明するといいよね。

Maybe it's good to explain what it is.

美しい雪の像が見られるよ。

You can see beautiful snow statues.

北海道に行ってみませんか。

Why don't you visit Hokkaido?

「Why don't you ~」で「～してみませんか」っていう意味だよ。

"Why don't you ~" means "~ *shite mimasenka.*"

あなたが好きなところを話してみて。

Why don't you talk about your favorite place?

京都は金閣寺で有名だよ。

Kyoto is famous for Kinkaku-ji.

金閣寺は金色で光っているよ。

It looks gold and shiny.

ぜひ京都に行ってみてね。

Why don't you visit Kyoto?

大阪はタコ焼きで有名です。

Osaka is famous for *Takoyaki.*

大阪にはたくさんのおいしいタコ焼き屋があります。

There are many delicious *Takoyaki* shops in Osaka.

ぜひ大阪に行ってみてね。

Why don't you visit Osaka?

兵庫は姫路城で有名だよ。

Hyogo is famous for Himeji Castle.

伝統的な日本の城だよ。

It is a traditional Japanese castle.

ぜひ兵庫に行ってみてね。

Why don't you visit Hyogo?

うん、そうだよね。

Oh, I see.

たくさんステキなところがあるね。

There are many cool places.

どこに行ってみたいですか？

Where do you want to visit?

3 投票する、手を挙げる

投票しよう。

Let's vote.

vote は「投票する」って意味だよ。

Vote means "*touhyou suru.*"

どこに行ってみたい？

Where do you want to go?

大阪に行きたい人？

Who wants to go to Osaka?

北海道に行きたい人は？

Who wants to go to Hokkaido?

そこで何をしてみたい？

What do you want to do there?

大阪に行って、タコ焼きを食べたい。

I want to go to Osaka to eat *Takoyaki*.

北海道に行って、雪を見たい。

I want to go to Hokkaido to see the snow.

15人の人が北海道に行きたいんだね。

Fifteen people want to go to Hokkaido.

一番人気のある場所は北海道だね。

The most popular place is Hokkaido.

4 好きな物、持ち物、ほしい物

カードを何枚か作って、好きな物やほしい物を発表しよう。

Let's make some cards to show what you like and what you want.

僕は動物が好きだよ。

I like animals.

ハムスターを飼っているよ。

I have a hamster.

犬がほしいよ。

I want a dog.

【I、like、have、want のカードを黒板に貼る】

僕は、

I,

like は「好き」って意味だよ。

Like means "*suki*."

have は「持っている」ってこと。

Have means "*motteiru.*"

---

want は「ほしい」とか「したい」ってことね。

Want means "*hoshii*" or "*shitai.*"

例を黒板に貼るから、自分の好きな物をカードに描いてね。

I'll put some examples on the blackboard, so draw your favorite things on the cards.

バナナが好きだよ。

I like bananas.

犬を飼っているよ。

I have a dog.

サッカーボールがほしいよ。

I want a soccer ball.

ネコが好きだよ。

I like cats.

ネコを飼っているよ。

I have a cat.

本がほしいよ。

I want a book.

単語を覚えましょう

●食べ物

すし	*sushi*	りんご	apple
ピザ	pizza	バナナ	banana
桃	peach	ピーナッツ	nut
魚	fish	スパゲッティ	spaghetti
ケーキ	cake	チョコレート	chocolate
アイスクリーム	ice cream		

●ペット

動物	animals	鳥	bird
犬	dog	ネコ	cat
ハムスター	hamster		

単語を覚えましょう

●持ち物、ほしい物

本	book
時計	watch
ケン玉	kendama
コンピューター	computer
野球のバット	baseball bat
サッカーボール	soccer ball
テニスのラケット	tennis racket
卓球のラケット	table tennis racket
バドミントンのラケット	badminton racket

5 自分の町について話そう（1）　　Track 84

僕たちの町を紹介しようね。

Let's introduce our town.

何があるかな？

What do we have?

美しい川があるよね。

We have a beautiful river.

図書館もあるね。

We also have a library.

これが僕たちの町の紹介の仕方だよ。

This is how to introduce our town.

これが僕の町だよ。

This is my town.

美しい山と川があります。

We have beautiful mountains and rivers.

ハイキングや魚釣りに行けるよ。

We can go hiking and fishing.

新しい図書館があります。

We have a new library.

図書館でたくさんの本を読んだり、勉強したりできるよ。

We can read many books and study in the library.

スイミングプールがあるよ。

We have a swimming pool.

一年中、泳げるよ。

We can swim all year long.

JR の駅と、神姫バスのターミナルがあるよ。

We have a JR station and a Shinki bus terminal.

電車やバスで他の場所へ行けるよ。

We can go to other places by train and bus.

市民病院があるよ。

We have a municipal hospital.

病気のときに、病院に行くことができるよ。

When we are sick, we can go to the hospital.

ゴルフ場があるよ。

We have golf courses.

映画館はないよ。

We don't have a movie theater.

これが僕の町だよ。

This is my town.

水族館があるよ。

We have an aquarium.

野球場があるよ。

We have a baseball stadium.

野球の試合を見られるよ。

We can watch baseball games.

JR の駅と地下鉄の駅があるよ。

We have a JR station and a subway station.

空港があるよ。

We have an airport.

毎日、多くの飛行機を見られるよ。

We can see many airplanes every day.

海があるよ。

We have an ocean.

たくさんの船を見られるよ。

We can see many ships.

自然はあまりないよ。

We don't have much nature.

古い神社があるよ。

We have an old shrine.

伝統的なお寺があるよ。

We have traditional temples.

有名な美術館があるよ。

We have a famous museum.

6 自分の町について話そう（2）　　Track 85

僕たちの町にないものについて、話をしましょう。

Let's talk about something we don't have in our town.

君の町に、もっと何がほしい？

What do you want more in your town?

映画館がほしいよ。

I want a movie theater.

どうして？　理由を教えて。

Why? Tell us the reason.

最新の映画を観られるから。

Because I can watch the latest movies.

遊園地がほしいよ。

I want an amusement park.

ジェットコースターに乗りたいから。

Because I want to ride a roller coaster.

サッカー場がほしいよ。

I want a soccer stadium.

サッカーをするのが好きだから。

Because I like playing soccer.

海水浴場がほしいよ。

I want a (swimming) beach.

泳ぐのが好きだから。

Because I like swimming.

ゴルフ場がほしいよ。

I want a golf course.

プロのゴルフ選手になりたいから。

Because I want to be a professional golf player.

スキー場がほしいよ。

I want ski slopes.

家族と一緒にスキーに行きたいから。

Because I want to go skiing with my family.

外国について話しましょう。
Let's talk about foreign countries.

foreign countries は「外国」って意味。
Foreign countries mean "*gaikoku.*"

どの国に興味がある？
What country are you interested in?

先生はカナダに興味があるよ。
I'm interested in Canada.

「ナイアガラの滝」が好きだから。
Because I like 'Niagara Falls.'

カナダでは英語とフランス語が話されているよ。
People speak English and French in Canada.

首都はオタワだよ。
The capital is Ottawa.

これがカナダの国旗だよ。
This is the Canadian flag.

赤と白だよ。
It is red and white.

赤いカエデの葉が旗の中央にあるよ。

A red maple leaf is in the center of the flag.

日本からカナダへは飛行機で９時間くらいだよ。

It is about 9 hours from Japan to Canada by airplane.

あなたの好きな国を教えて。

Tell me your favorite country.

それと理由を教えてね。

And tell me the reason.

僕は韓国に興味があるよ。

I'm interested in Korea.

Ｋポップが好きだから。

Because I like K-POP.

韓国では韓国語が話されているよ。

People speak Korean in Korea.

韓国の首都はソウルだよ。

The capital of Korea is Seoul.

これが韓国の国旗だよ。

This is the Korean flag.

赤、青、黒と白だよ。

It is red, blue, black and white.

日本から韓国へは飛行機で2時間くらいだよ。

It is about 2 hours from Japan to Korea by airplane.

8 小学校生活の思い出 Track 87

あなたの一番の思い出は何？

What's your best memory?

一番の思い出は運動会だよ。

My best memory is sports day.

一番の思い出は、もちつき大会だよ。

My best memory is the *mochi* making festival.

一番の思い出はマラソンだよ。

My best memory is the marathon.

以前にあったことを話すときは過去形を使うんだったよね。

Use past tense when you talk about something has happened.

例えば、音楽会が楽しかったよ。

For example, I enjoyed the music festival.

水泳大会が楽しかったよ。

I enjoyed the swimming meet.

英語の授業が楽しかったよ。

I enjoyed the English class.

遠足がすばらしかったよ。

The field trip was great.

給食がすばらしかったよ。

The school lunch was great.

清掃の日がすばらしかったよ。

The cleaning day was great.

修学旅行が一番良かったよ。

I liked the school trip the best.

休み時間が一番好きだったよ。

I liked recess the best.

参観日が一番好きだったよ。

I liked the open school the best.

運動会はどんなふうに良かったの？

How did you like sports day?

かけっこで1位になったよ。

I won the race.

もちつき大会はどんなふうに良かったの？

How did you like the *mochi* making festival?

きな粉もちがおいしかったよ。

Kinako-mochi was yummy.

マラソンはどんなふうに良かったの？

How did you like the marathon?

3位になったよ。

I won third place.

音楽会はどうだった？

How was the music festival?

リコーダーの演奏が楽しかったよ。

I enjoyed playing the recorder.

水泳大会はどうだった？

How was the swimming meet?

泳ぐのが楽しかったよ。

I enjoyed swimming.

英語の授業はどうだった？

How was the English class?

英語の歌を歌うのが楽しかったよ。

I enjoyed singing English songs.

遠足のことを詳しく教えて。

Tell me more about the field trip.

公園からの景色がきれいだったよ。

The view from the park was beautiful.

給食のことを詳しく教えて。

Tell me more about the school lunch.

カレーライスが大好きだったよ。

I loved curry and rice.

清掃の日のことをもっと教えて。

Tell me more about the cleaning day.

運動場の掃除をしたよ。

We cleaned the ground.

どうして修学旅行が一番良かったの？

Why did you like the school trip the best?

家族におみやげをたくさん買えたから。

Because I bought a lot of souvenirs for my family.

どうして休み時間が一番良かったの？

Why did you like recess the best?

友だちとしゃべるのが楽しかったから。

Because I enjoyed talking to my friends.

どうして参観日が一番良かったの？

Why did you like the open school?

お母さんが学校に来てくれたから。

Because my mother came to school.

いいね。

Sounds good.

楽しそうだね！

Sounds like fun!

すばらしいね！

That's great!

9　将来の夢や職業　　　　　　　　　Track 88

将来、何になりたい？

What do you want to be in the future?

先生になりたい。

I want to be a teacher.

どうやったら先生になれるかな？

How can you be a teacher?

学校に行く。

I go to school.

何をするの？

What do you do?

がんばって勉強する。
I'll study hard.

小児科医になりたい。
I want to be a children's doctor.

歯医者になりたい。
I want to be a dentist.

看護師になりたい。
I want to be a nurse.

パン屋になりたい。
I want to be a baker.

声優になりたい。
I want to be a voice actor.

マンガ家になりたい。
I want to be a *manga* artist.

絵本作家になりたい。
I want to be a picture book author.

イラストレーターになりたい。
I want to be an illustrator.

警察官になりたい。
I want to be a police officer.

消防士になりたい。

I want to be a firefighter.

プロサッカー選手になりたい。

I want to be a professional soccer player.

プロ野球選手になりたい。

I want to be a professional baseball player.

プロテニス選手になりたい。

I want to be a professional tennis player.

動物園の飼育員になりたい。

I want to be a zookeeper.

バスの運転手になりたい。

I want to be a bus driver.

ウーバーの運転手になりたい。

I want to be an Uber driver.

パイロットになりたい。

I want to be a pilot.

単語を覚えましょう

●職業

教師	teacher	医者	doctor
警察官	police officer	歯医者	dentist
パン屋	baker	看護士	nurse
店員	salesclerk	デザイナー	designer
運転手	driver	弁護士	lawyer
パイロット	pilot	消防士	firefighter

Part 4

先生と生徒の
コミュニケーション

1 語りかける

やぁ、みんな。
Hey, class.

みんな、聞こえる？
Can you all hear?

みんな、見える？
Can everybody see?

大丈夫？
Are you OK?

まぁ、いいとして。
Oh, well.

えっと。
Well.

あれ、知らない？
Oh, you don't know?

終わった？
Have you finished?

手を挙げてね。

Please raise your hand.

2 確認する　　　　　　　　　　　　　　Track 90

本当に？

Really?

そう？

Is it?

そうなの？

You do?

君は？

How about you?

君はどう？

What about you?

やってみない？

Why don't you try?

〜の答えは？

What's the answer to ~ ?

そうなの？

Is that right?

わかった？
Do you understand?

わかった？
Understand?

わかった？
Got it?

先生の言うこと、わかった？
Are you with me?

言うこと、わかった？
Did you get the message?

見つかった？
Did you find it?

わかった？
Have you got it?

3 依頼する
Track 91

～してくれる？
Could you ~ ?

黒板をきれいにしてくれる？
Could you clean the blackboard, please?

知らせて。

Let me know.

手を挙げてね。

Please raise your hand.

もう少し大きな声で言ってね。

Say it louder, please.

4 発言を促す   Track 92

どう思う？

What do you think?

あなたの意見は？

What's your opinion?

何かない？

Anything?

あなたの答えは？

What's your answer?

誰かやってみたい人？

Any volunteers?

誰かやってみたい人？

Who wants to try?

目を合わせて。

Make eye contact.

恥ずかしがらないで。

Don't be shy.

ちょっと落ち着こう。

Let's take a moment.

「無理」って言わないで。

Don't say, *"Muri."*

絶対に「無理」って言わないで。

Never say, *"Muri."*

どんな答えでもいいよ。

Any answer will be fine.

どんな答えでも大丈夫だよ。

Any answer will be OK.

どんな答えでもいいよ。

Any answer is good.

何か言ってみて。

Just say something.

挑戦してみて。

Give it a try.

やってみて。

Give it a shot.

どうぞ。

Go ahead.

6 注意する　　　　　　　　　　　　　　Track 94

そんなに大声で言わないで。

Don't be so loud.

静かにして。

Be quiet.

じゃましないで。

Don't interrupt.

顔を上げて。

Face up.

何をしているの？

What are you doing?

やめなさい。

Stop it.

まっすぐ座りなさい。

Sit up, straight.

7 ほめる Track 95

【よくできている子をほめる】

すばらしい！

Great!

すばらしいよ！

You are doing great!

すばらしいよ！

You are brilliant!

すばらしい！

You did a great job!

すばらしい！

Fantastic!

完璧！

Perfect!

最高！

Excellent!

すばらしい！
Wonderful!

すごい！
Super!

おめでとう！
Congratulations!

【普通にほめる】

いいね！
Nice!

いいね！
Good!

いい考えだね！
Good idea!

上手にできているよ。
You're doing well.

その通り！
That's right!

その通り！
That's it!

正解！
Correct!

よくできました。
Well done.

よくできました。
Good job.

惜しい！
Nice try!

手伝ってくれてありがとう。
Thank you for helping me.

ユミちゃんを手伝ってくれてありがとう。
Thank you for helping Yumi.

8 励ます Track 96

【できていない子を励ます】

あきらめないで。
Don't give up.

気にしなくていいよ。
Don't worry.

恥ずかしがらないで。

Don't be shy.

誰でも失敗はするよ。

Everybody makes mistakes.

誰でも失敗するよ。

Everyone makes mistakes.

大丈夫だよ。

That's OK.

それでいいよ。

That's good.

がんばったね。

Nice try.

よくがんばったよ。

Good try.

惜しい。

Close.

惜しい！

Almost!

すごく惜しい。

You are so close.

その調子。
Keep it up.

もう一度やってみて。
Try again.

もう一度それをやってみて。
Try it again.

もう一度言ってみて。
Say it again.

もう一度。
One more time.

次はきっとできるよ。
I'm sure you can do it next time.

【時間のかかる子を励ます】

手伝ってほしい？
Do you need help?

もっと時間がいる？
Do you need more time?

手伝おうか？
May I help you?

手伝おうか？
Can I help you?

先生に手伝ってほしい？
Do you want me to help you?

できるよ！
You can do it!

やってみてごらん。
Why don't you try?

落ち着いて。
Take it easy.

落ち着いて。
Relax.

焦らないで、ゆっくりやってみて。
Take your time.

見せて。
Show me yours.

次の、できる？
Can you do the next one?

自分がやっていることに集中して。
Concentrate on your work.

上手になってきたよ。

You are doing better.

9 あいづちを打つ

いいね。

Cool.

やったね！

Fabulous!

すごい。

Awesome.

信じられない。

Unbelievable.

とてもおもしろい。

Hilarious.

ふむふむ。

Uh-huh.

いいね。

Nice.

10 聞き返す

何？

Pardon?

何？

Pardon me?

もう一回、言って。

I beg your pardon?

もう一度、言ってくれる？

Would you say that again?

〈参考〉

「　　　」って言ったの？

You said, "　　　", right?

「　　　」ということ？

You mean, "　　　"?

えっと、
Well,

えっと、
Let me see,

えっと、
Let's see,

えっと、
Let me think,

では、
So,

ところで、
By the way,

とにかく、
Anyway,

でしょう、
You know,

そして、
And,

さらに、
Besides,

でも、
But,

でも、
However,

でも、
Though,

なぜなら、
Because,

なぜなら、
As,

または、
Or,

まとめると、
In short,

さもないと、
Otherwise,

一方、
On the other hand,

生徒が使う表現

1 楽しかったとき

楽しかった。

It was fun.

すごく楽しかった。

I had a great time.

本当に楽しかった。

I really enjoyed it.

おもしろい授業だった。

It was an interesting lesson.

次の授業が待ちきれない。

I can't wait for the next lesson.

次の授業が楽しみ。

I'm looking forward to the next lesson.

2 わからないとき   Track 101

わからなかった。
I didn't understand.

聞こえなかった。
I couldn't hear.

わからなかった。
I didn't get it.

3 道具がないとき   Track 102

エンピツを持っていない。
I don't have a pencil.

エンピツをなくした。
I lost my pencil.

エンピツが見つからない。
I can't find my pencil.

4 パートナーがいないとき

パートナーがいない。

I don't have a partner.

パートナーが見つからない。

I can't find a partner.

パートナーがいなくなった。

I'm missing my partner.

パートナーがいなくなった。

I lost my partner.

5 体調が悪いとき

気分が良くない。

I don't feel good.

気分が悪い。

I feel sick.

クラクラする。

I'm dizzy.

頭痛がする。

I have a headache.

単語を覚えましょう

●体の部位

顔	face	体	body
頭	head	肩	shoulder
髪	hair	首	neck
目	eye	手	hand
耳	ear	腕	arm
鼻	nose	足	foot
唇	lip	脚	leg

Part 5

学習指導編

チェックテストをする

「run」の意味は何？
What does "run" mean?

「うれしい」は英語で何て言うの？
How do you say *"ureshii"* in English?
— Happy.

その通り！
That's right!

よく覚えてるね。
You remember very well.

「listen」は日本語で何て言うの？
How do you say "listen" in Japanese?
— *Kiku.*

黒板の単語が見える？
Can you see the word on the blackboard?

このカードを見て。
Look at this card.

意味はわかる？

Do you know the meaning?

この単語の意味を知ってる？

Do you know the meaning of this word?

辞書を使って。

Use your dictionary.

質問はある？

Do you have any questions?

2 フレーズの確認をする　　　　　Track 106

フレーズを確認しよう。

Check these phrases.

このフレーズはわかるかな？

Do you know this phrase?

意味はわかるかな？

Do you know the meaning?

このフレーズを覚えて。

Memorize this phrase.

この文を覚えて。

Memorize this sentence.

お腹が空いているとき、何て言う？

When you are hungry, what would you say?

絵を見て。

Look at the picture.

女の子は何て言っている？

What does the girl say?

もし友だちが「Thank you」と言ったら、あなたは何て言う？

If your friend says "Thank you," what would you say?

どういたしまして。

You're welcome.

もし先生が「How are you?」と言ったら、あなたは何て言う？

If your teacher says "How are you?", what would you say?

元気です、ありがとう。

I'm fine, thank you.

3 リスニングテストをする   Track 107

リスニングテスト〔クイズ〕をするね。

I'll give you a listening test〔quiz〕.

10問のテスト〔クイズ〕をするね。

I'll give you a ten-question test 〔quiz〕.

CDを聞いて、質問に答えてね。

Listen to the CD and answer the questions.

プリントの正しい絵に〇をつけてね。

Circle the correct picture on your paper.

よく聞いて、正しい単語を選びなさい。

Listen carefully and choose the correct words.

聞いて、番号を書いて。

Listen and write the number.

もう一度聞きたい？

Do you want to listen again?

ヒントがほしい人？

Who needs a hint? * clue（ヒント）も使われます。

難しすぎる？

Is it too difficult?

できるよ。

You can do it.

もう一度よく聞いてみて。

Listen carefully one more time.

文章を暗記した？

Did you memorize the sentences?

がんばって練習してきた？

Did you practice hard?

もっと時間がいる？

Do you need more time?

まず、みんなで練習してみよう。

Let's practice together first.

確認するね。

Let me check.

始めて。

Please begin.

聞いているよ。

I'm listening.

忘れちゃった？

You forgot?

もっと練習しないとね。

You need more practice.

次の人、どうぞ。

Next person, please.

上手にできたね！

Good job!

大きな声で（はっきりと）。

Speak up.

速すぎるよ。

Too fast.

遅すぎるよ。

Too slow.

友だちとお互いにチェックして。

Ask your friend to check each other.

5 単語テストをする   Track 109

【黒板を使って単語を選ぶ（書く）】

黒板の絵を見て。

Look at the picture on the board.

正しい単語を選べる？〔カードで〕

Can you choose the right word?

隣に単語を書ける？

Can you spell the word next to it?

やってみたい人？

Any volunteers?

では、グループを作って。

Now, make a group.

リーダーを選んで。

Choose a leader.

リーダーがチームのみんなに絵カードを見せて、みんなは正しいカードを選ぼう。

The leader will show the picture card and members should choose the right card.

どのチームがカードを一番多く取れたかな？

Which team got the most cards?

誰が一番多く書けたかな？

Who wrote the most words?

【各自が紙で書く】

紙の絵を見て。

Look at the picture on the paper.

正しい単語を選べるかな？

Can you choose the right word?

隣に単語を書ける？

Can you spell the word next to it?

もし難しすぎたら、黒板を見て、写して。

If it is too difficult, look at the board and copy it.

時間がかかってもいいよ。

Take your time.

書き終わったら、名前を書いて、前に持って来て。

When you finish it, write your name and bring it to the front.

今度は、5問のテストをするね。

This time, I'll give you a five-question test.

準備はいい？

Are you ready?

5分でやってね。

I'll give you five minutes.

始めて。

Please begin.

終わりだよ。

Time is up.

隣の人と紙を交換して。

Switch your sheet with the person next to you.

答えを確認して。

Check your answers.

満点の人？

Who got a perfect score?

4 点の人？

Who got four points?

3 点の人？

Who got three points?

2 点の人？

Who got two points?

1 点の人？

Who got one point?

0 点の人？

Who got zero points?

次はがんばってね。

Try harder next time.

6 書き取りテストをする   Track 110

では、書き取りの練習をするよ。

Now, we will have dictation practice.

よく聞いてね。

Listen carefully.

"red" "r, e, d"

終わった？

Finished?

黒板を見て。

Look at the blackboard.

確認するね。

Let me check.

よくできました。

Good job.

次は、書き取りのテストをするね。

Next, we will have a dictation test.

"I like red."
"I like blue."

テキスト・辞書・宿題について

1 テキストの使い方を説明する   Track 111

これが教科書だよ。

This is your textbook.

教科書の裏に名前を書いた？

Did you write your name on the back of the textbook?

英語で（名前を）書いてね。

Write your name in English.

アルファベットで（名前を）書いてね。

Write your name in alphabet.

ローマ字で（名前を）書いてね。

Write your name in Roma-ji.

表紙を見て。

Look at the cover.

何て書いてある？

What does it say?

教科書を開いて。

Open your textbook.

目次を確認しよう。

Let's check the contents.

ユニット1はあいさつについてだよ。

Unit 1 is about greetings.

ユニット2は季節についてだよ。

Unit 2 is about seasons.

ユニット3はスポーツについてだよ。

Unit 3 is about sports.

50ページ以降は、絵カードだよ。

After page 50, they are picture cards.

絵カードを切って、関連のあるユニットで使うよ。

We'll cut them out and use them in a specific unit.

2 辞書の使い方を説明する　　　　　　　Track 112

これが辞書だよ。

This is a dictionary.

「英和」は英語から日本語だよ。

***"Eiwa"* means English-Japanese.**

「和英」は日本語から英語だよ。

***"Waei"* means Japanese-English.**

英語の単語を調べたいときは、「英和」を使ってね。

When you want to check English words, use *"Eiwa."*

日本語から英語を調べたいときは、「和英」を使ってね。

When you want to look up a Japanese word to English, use *"Waei."*

【英和辞典を使って調べる】

例えば、「flag」を探したいなら、

For example, if you want to look up "flag",

まず、「f」を見つけて。

Find "f", first.

見つかった？

Did you find it?

次に、「l」を見つけて。

Next, find "l."

アルファベットの順番だよ。

They are in alphabetical order.

次は、「a」ね。

Next, "a."

最後は「g」ね。

The last one is "g."

「flag」は見つかった？

Did you find "flag"?

それはどういう意味？

What does it mean?

「旗」

"*Hata.*"

【和英辞典を使って調べる】

では「和英」で「赤」を見つけて。

Now find *"aka"* in *"Waei."*

国語の辞書を使うみたいに単語を調べてね。

You can look up the word like using a Japanese dictionary.

見つかった？

Did you find it?

それはどういう意味？

What does it mean?

「赤」

"Red."

3 宿題を出す

これは宿題だよ。

This is your homework.

毎日、歌を聞いてきてね。

Listen to the song every day.

家で「ABC ソング」を 5 回、歌ってきてね。

Sing "the ABC song" 5 times at home.

家で自分の名前を英語で 10 回、書いてきてね。

Write your name in English 10 times at home.

毎日、自己紹介の練習をしてね。

Practice introduction every day.

家族に何才か聞いてきてね。

Ask your family how old they are.

次の授業までに DVD を 5 回、観てきてね。

Watch the DVD 5 times before the next lesson.

来週までに CD を 5 回、聞いてきてね。

Listen to the CD 5 times before next week.

宿題のプリントをやってきてね。

Complete the homework sheet.

次の授業までにユニット 3 を読んできてね。

Read Unit 3 before the next lesson.

テストについて説明する

1 単語テスト

単語テストをするよ。

I'll give you a vocabulary test.

テスト用紙を見てね。

Look at the test sheet.

5つの絵があるよ。

There are five pictures.

その単語を英語で書いてね。

Write the words in English.

次に、英単語が5つあるよ。

Next, there are five English words.

日本語で意味を書いてね。

Write the meaning in Japanese.

【単語テスト終了後】

終わった？

Are you done?

用紙を集めるね。
I'll collect your sheet.

来週、用紙を返すね。
I'll give them back next week.

2 リスニングテスト　　　　　　　　　　　Track 115

リスニングテストをするよ。
I'll give you a listening test.

リスニングクイズをするよ。
I'll give you a listening quiz.

よく聞いてね。
Listen carefully.

用紙に 2 つの絵があるよ。
There are two pictures on the sheet.

CD を聞いたあとに、正しいほうの絵を選んでね。
After you listen to the CD, choose the right one.

入力欄に○を書いてね。
Write a circle in the box.

5 問あるよ。
There are five questions.

準備はいいかな？

Are you ready?

【リスニングテスト終了後】

終わった？

Are you done?

用紙を集めるね。

I'll collect your sheet.

来週、用紙を返すね。

I'll give them back next week.

3 ディクテーション〔書き取り〕テスト　　Track 116

ディクテーションテストをするよ。

I'll give you a dictation test.

よく聞いてね。

Listen carefully.

CD を聞いて、彼が言ったことを（紙に）書いてね。

Listen to the CD, and write what he said.

5問あるよ。

There are five questions.

準備はいいかな？

Are you ready?

【ディクテーションテスト終了後】

終わった？

Are you done?

用紙を集めるね。

I'll collect your sheet.

来週、用紙を返すね。

I'll give them back next week.

Part 6

発展編

ペアワーク、グループワーク

1 ペア、グループを作る   Track 117

ペアを作って。
Make pairs.

パートナーを見つけて。
Find your partner.

ペアがいない人は、手を挙げてね。
If you don't find a pair, raise your hand.

ペアで活動して。
Work in pairs.

パートナーと向き合って。
Face your partner.

お互いに向き合って。
Face each other.

4人のグループを作って。
Make groups of four.

各グループに4人ずつね。
Four students should be in each group.

このグループは 1 人足りない？
Is this group missing one student?

じゃあ、先生がこのグループに入るね。
Then, I'll be on your team.

このグループは 2 人足りないの？
Is this group missing two students?

あのグループは 2 人足りない？
Is that group missing two students?

じゃあ、一緒に 1 つのグループにしよう。
Then, let's make a group together.

2 人数を確認する Track 118

今日は何人いる？
How many people are there today?

みんなで数えてみよう。
Let's count together.

1、2、3…24。
One, two, three … twenty-four.

全部で 24 人だね。
Twenty-four in total.

自分のグループの人数を数えて。

Count the members of your group.

多すぎたり、少なすぎたりしたら、先生に知らせて。

If there are too many or few, please let me know.

3 発表者を決める   Track 119

グループで話し合って。

Talk in your group.

グループ内でリーダーを決めて。

Make a leader in your group.

誰が発表する？

Who is going to present the speech?

誰が写真を見せる？

Who is going to show the picture?

誰がボードを動かす？

Who is going to move the board?

誰がプリントを配る？

Who is going to hand out?

4 ペア、グループを代える

パートナーを代えよう。

Let's change partners.

新しいパートナーを見つけて。

Find a new partner.

歩き回って、新しいパートナーを見つけて。

Walk around to find a new partner.

まだ新しいパートナーを探している人？

Who is still looking for a new partner?

同じ相手を選んではダメだよ。

Don't choose the same partner.

5人のグループを作って。

Make groups of five.

このグループには7人いるよ。

Seven people are in this group.

先生と一緒に2人来て。

Two should come with me.

このグループは、あと3人探しているよ。

This group is looking for three more members.

来て、このグループに入って。

Come and join this group.

円になって。

Make a circle.

各グループで円になって。

Each group should make a circle.

隣同士、近づいて座って。

Sit close to each other.

誰が最初にする？

Who's first?

順番を決めましょう。

Let's decide the order.

じゃんけんぽん、1、2、3。

Rock, paper, scissors, one, two, three.

あなたが1番目ね。

You are (the) first.

あなたが2番目ね。

You are second.

あなたが3番目ね。

You are third.

あなたが4番目ね。

You are forth.

7 理解度を確認する　　　　　　　　　　　Track 123

わかった？

Do you understand?

もっと説明が必要な人？

Who needs more explanation?

わかったら、手を挙げてね。

If you understand, please raise your hand.

わからなかったら、手を挙げてね。

If you don't understand, please raise your hand.

誰か、ミホちゃんを助けてあげてくれる？

Can anyone help Miho?

あと 2 分ね。

You have two minutes left.

もっと時間が必要？

Do you need more time?

あと 1 分ね。

I'll give you one more minute.

時間が来たよ。

Time is up.

単語を覚えましょう

●時、時間

朝	morning	今日	today
昼	noon	明日	tomorrow
夜	night	昨日	yesterday
1時	one o'clock	7時	seven o'clock
2時	two o'clock	8時	eight o'clock
3時	three o'clock	9時	nine o'clock
4時	four o'clock	10時	ten o'clock
5時	five o'clock	11時	eleven o'clock
6時	six o'clock	12時	twelve o'clock

Part 6

発展編

発表する〔プレゼンテーションに繋げる〕

1 自分の意見を言う   Track 125

プレゼンに挑戦しよう。

Let's try a presentation.

プレゼンをするのって楽しいよ。

It's fun to give a presentation.

プレゼンって知ってるかな？

Do you know the presentation?

プレゼンというのは、自分の考えやアイデアをみんなの前で発表すること
だよ。

**A presentation is to show your thoughts and ideas in
front of other people.**

資料を引用すると、役に立つよ。

If you use some documents, it's helpful.

資料を引用したら、「～から引用です」と言ってね。

**When you use some documents, you should say, "I got
this idea from ~."**

発表するときは、はっきりと話そうね。

When you give a presentation, you should speak clearly.

理由も付け加えようね。

You should add some reasons.

例えば、こんなふうに言いたいなら…、

For example, if you want to say…,

私は〜が好きだよ。

I like ~.

私は晴れの日が好きだよ。

I like sunny days.

他の言い方もあるよ。

There is another way to say.

私は〜と思うよ。

I think ~.

私は、晴れの日が一番だと思うよ。

I think sunny days are the best.

私の意見は〜です。

My opinion is ~.

私の意見は、晴れの日が一番です。

My opinion is that sunny days are the best.

私は〜だと思います。

I believe that ~.

私は、晴れの日が一番だと思います。

I believe that sunny days are the best.

では、理由を足しましょう。

Now, add some reasons.

reason は「理由」と言う意味だよ。

Reason means "*riyu.*"

まず、

First,

一番目に、きれいな空を見ることができます。

First, we can see the beautiful sky.

beautiful sky は「美しい空」という意味だよ。

Beautiful sky means "*utsukushii sora.*"

次に、

Second,

2番目に、外で遊べます。

Second, we can play outside.

second は「2番目に」という意味だよ。

Second means "*nibanmeni.*"

outside は「外」と言う意味だよ。

Outside means "*soto.*"

3つ目に、

Third,

3つ目に、サッカーをするのが好きです。

Third, I like playing soccer.

それで、

So,

それで、私は晴れの日が一番だと思います。

So, I think sunny days are the best.

わかった？

Do you understand?

2 資料を引用する　　　　　　　Track 126

何か資料を見つけましょう。

Let's find some documents.

たぶん新聞がいいと思うよ。

Maybe newspaper is good.

〜によると、

According to ~,

今日の新聞によると、

According to today's newspaper,

~には、
In ~,

今日の新聞には、
In today's newspaper,

~を読むと、
I read ~,

今日の新聞を読むと、
I read today's newspaper,

今日の新聞によると、晴れた日に外で遊ぶことが子供たちにとっては最も良いそうです。
According to today's newspaper, playing outside on a sunny day is the best for children.

今日の新聞を読むと、子供たちはもっと外で遊ぶべきだそうです。
I read today's newspaper, children should play outside more often.

今日の新聞からこのアイデアを思いつきました。
I got this idea from today's newspaper.

例えば、20年前はもっとたくさんの子供たちが外で遊んでいたそうですよ。
For example, more children played outside 20 years ago.

子供たちはとても元気でした。
They were very healthy.

ハナさんが言うように、子供たちはもっと活発であるべきですね。

As Hana said, children should be more active.

3 発表でよく使う表現 Track 127

【付け加えるとき】

もしアイデアを付け加えたいなら、「Also」と言ってね。

If you want to add an idea, say "Also."

また、

Also,

また、晴れた日にはドッジボールもできます。

Also, we can play dodgeball on a sunny day.

それだけではなく、

Not only that,

それだけではなく、鬼ごっこもできます。

Not only that, we can play tag.

【比較するとき】

もし何かと比べたいときは、「Compared to ～」と言ってね。

If you want to compare something, say "Compared to ~."

雨の日に比べて、私たちは活動的になれます。

Compared to a rainy day, we can be active.

【結論を述べるとき】

もしまとめを言いたいときは、「So」と言ってね。

If you want to conclude, say "So."

それで、私は晴れの日が好きです。

So, I like sunny days.

それで、私は晴れの日が一番だと思います。

So, I think sunny days are the best.

単語を覚えましょう			
●天気			
晴れた	sunny	雨の	rainy
曇った	cloudy	風がある	windy
●気候			
暑い	hot	寒い	cold
暖かい	warm	涼しい	cool

3 討論する〔ディベート〕

ディベートに挑戦しよう。

Let's try a debate.

ディベートって知ってる？

Do you know about debates?

ディベートというのは論理的な話し合いだよ。

A debate is a discussion that happens logically.

自分の見方や意見を表現してね。

Express your views or opinions.

質問してもいいよ。

You can ask questions too.

ルールはこのような感じ。

These are the rules.

まず、テーマを選んで、自分がその意見に賛成か反対かを決めます。

First, we have to choose a theme and decide if you agree or disagree with the idea.

次に、チームに分かれ、それぞれのチームは情報を集めます。

Second, make teams and each team gathers some information.

3番目に、質問されたときは、答えを準備しておかなければなりません。

Third, you have to prepare your answers for when you are asked questions.

これは例だよ。

This is an example.

テーマは「晴れの日の遊び」についてです。

The theme is "How to play on a sunny day."

もし晴れた日に外で遊びたいなら、何をしたいか、そしてどうしてそう思うのか？

If you want to play outside on a sunny day, what would you do and why do you think so?

晴れたら、外で遊びたいよ。

On a sunny day, I want to play outside.

ドッジボールがしたいよ、理由はドッジボールが好きだから。

I want to play dodgeball because I like dodgeball.

晴れた日には、外で遊びたいよ。

On a sunny day, I would like to play outside.

サッカーがしたいよ、理由はサッカーが好きだから。

I want to play soccer because I like soccer.

ドッジボールについて質問があるよ。

I have a question about dodgeball.

サッカーについて聞きたいよ。

I would like to ask you about soccer.

ルールについて、もう少し教えて。

Tell me more about the rules.

ボールについて、どう思う？

What do you think about the ball?

意見を聞かせてくれる？

May I ask your opinion?

これについて、どうですか？

What's your take on this?

あなたの意見は？

What's your opinion?

2 相手の発言を引用する　　　　Track 129

~と言ったよね？
You said ~?

晴れの日が一番だと言いました。
You said sunny days are the best.

20年前はもっとたくさんの子供が外で遊んでいたとあなたは思うのですね。
You think more children played outside 20 years ago.

外で遊ぶのがいいということですね。
You mean playing outside is good.

3 相手の意見を求める　　　　Track 130

室内で遊ぶことについて、どう思いますか？
What do you think about playing inside?

室内で遊びたい人もいると思いますか？
Do you think some people want to play inside?

外で遊ぶと皮膚に悪いと思いませんか？
Don't you think playing outside is bad for the skin?

【より詳しい説明を求める】

あなたの体験をもっと聞かせて。

Tell me more about your experience.

ルールについて、もう少し知っていますか？

Do you know more about the rules?

ルールについて、もっと知りたいです。

I want to know more about the rules.

【より詳しい説明をする】

私は毎日、友だちとサッカーと鬼ごっこをします。

I enjoy playing soccer and tag with my friends every day.

図書館に行けば、その本を読むことができます。

You can go to the library to read books.

かくれんぼ、キックベースボールと縄跳びはいいと思います。

I think hide and seek, kick baseball and jump rubber are good.

【相手に賛成するとき】

私はあなたに賛成です。
I agree with you.

私もそう思います。
I think so too.

【相手に反論するとき】

私は反対です。
I disagree.

私はそう思いません。
I don't think so.

5 まとめる   Track 132

多数決で決めましょう。
Let's decide by majority vote.

多数決を取りましょう。
Let's take a vote.

手を挙げてください。
Raise your hand.

晴れの日に外で遊ぶのが好きな人は？

Who likes to play outside on a sunny day?

雨の日に中で遊ぶのが好きな人は？

Who likes to play inside on a rainy day?

5人が晴れの日に外で遊びたい。

Five people like to play outside on a sunny day.

3人が雨の日に中で遊びたい。

Three people like to play inside on a rainy day.

晴れの日にはドッジボールをします。

We will play dodgeball on a sunny day.

雨の日には読書をします。

We will read books on a rainy day.

単語を覚えましょう

●月

1 月	January	7 月	July
2 月	February	8 月	August
3 月	March	9 月	September
4 月	April	10 月	October
5 月	May	11 月	November
6 月	June	12 月	December

●曜日

月曜日	Monday	金曜日	Friday
火曜日	Tuesday	土曜日	Saturday
水曜日	Wednesday	日曜日	Sunday
木曜日	Thursday		

Part 6

発展編

Part 7

ALT との会話

1 ALT と打ち合わせをする

1 電話で事前に打ち合わせをする　　　Track 133

もしもし。ABC 小学校の田中と申します。

Hello. This is Tanaka from ABC Elementary School.

一緒にティーム・ティーチングをさせていただきます。

I'm your team-teaching partner.

封筒を受け取りましたか？

Have you received the envelope?

明日は３クラスあります。

We will have three classes tomorrow.

８時 30 分に職員室に来てくださいますか？

Will you come to the teachers' office at 8:30?

2 出迎える　　　Track 134

はじめまして。

Nice to meet you.

お元気ですか？

How are you?

お会いできるのを楽しみにしていました。

We were looking forward to meeting you.

来てくれてありがとうございます。

Thank you for coming.

3 紹介する

田中です。

I'm Tanaka.

よろしくお願いします。

Nice to meet you.

こちらは教頭の上田先生です。

This is the vice principal, Mr. Ueda.

4 連絡事項を伝える

授業が終わったら、職員室に来てください。

After finishing your class, please come to the teachers' office.

Part 7

ＡＬＴとの会話

【教育方針について】

本校の教育方針は自主性です。

The goal of our school is Independence.

【学校行事について】

これが本校の年間行事予定です。

This is the annual schedule of our school.

これが毎月の予定です。

This is our monthly schedule.

【教科外活動について】

4年生は1学期に野外活動に行きます。

The 4th graders will go on field activities during the first term.

6 授業計画 Track 138

私たちの授業は文部科学省の定めた学習指導要領に基づいています。

Our lessons are based on the course of study as proclaimed by the Ministry of Education, Culture, Sports, Science and Technology.

コミュニケーションスキルとして英語を教えることが大切です。

It is important to teach English as a communication skill.

7 ティーム・ティーチング Track 139

ティーム・ティーチングでは、聞くことと話すことに重点を置きたいと思っています。

In team teaching, I'd like to emphasize listening and speaking.

日本語は話さないでほしいです。

I'd like you not to speak any Japanese.

2 ALT と授業をする

1 授業の依頼をする   Track 140

単発の授業をお願いできますか？

Would you have a one-shot visit〔lesson〕?

生徒のために簡単なゲームを準備してもらえますか？

Would you prepare an easy game for the students?

これを使ってもらえますか？

Would you use this?

このカードはとても便利です。

These cards are very useful.

英語の歌を歌ってもらえますか？

Would you sing an English song?

2 提示する   Track 141

この授業の指導の役割分担を話し合って決めておきましょう。

We should discuss how we should divide the teaching role for this lesson.

あなたとレッスンプランについて意見を出し合って、必要なときは変更を
したいと思っています。

I'd like to discuss the lesson plan with you and change it if needed.

---

3 指示を出す

クラスの生徒にあいさつをしてもらえますか？

Would you greet the class?

先週末をどのように過ごしたか、生徒に話してもらえますか？

Would you tell them how you spent last weekend?

簡単な英語で生徒に指示を出してもらえませんか？

Would you give a direction to the students using simple English?

もう少し簡単にしてもらえますか？

Would you make it easier?

生徒たちに簡単な対話文〔ダイアローグ〕を作ってもらえませんか？

Would you make a simple dialogue for the students? もし
生徒が理解できなければ、私が日本語で説明します。

If the students don't understand you, I'll explain in Japanese.

3-2 の生徒はおとなしく、授業中にあまり発表をしません。

The students of 3-2 are rather quiet and don't express themselves during class.

あなたのふるさとについて聞かせてくださいますか？

Would you tell us about your hometown?

個人的なことを聞いてもいいですか？

May I ask you a personal question?

このレッスンについて率直なご意見をいただけませんか？

Would you give me a frank comment on this lesson?

もう一度、説明してもらえますか？

Would you explain it again?

もう一度、言ってもらえますか？
I beg your pardon?

もう一度、繰り返してもらえますか？
Would you repeat it again?

6 感謝する

歌ってくれてありがとうございます。
Thank you for singing.

当校に来てくださってありがとうございます。
Thank you for coming to our school.

授業をしてくださってありがとうございました。
Thank you for the lesson.

7 終了を告げる

そろそろ授業が終わります。
It's about time to finish this lesson.

Part 7

ALTとの会話

Part 8

学校生活編

学校を案内する

1 校内を説明する

これは事務室です。

This is the secretary's office.

あれは生徒用の玄関です。

That is the students' entrance.

コンピュータ室を使ってください。

Please use the computer room.

校長先生は校長室にいらっしゃいます。

The principal is in the principal's room.

教頭先生は職員室にいらっしゃいます。

The vice principal is in the teachers' room.

担任の先生は教室にいらっしゃいます。

The homeroom teacher is in the classroom.

体育館へ行かれますか？

Would you like to go to the gym?

生徒たちを図書室へ連れて行ってくれますか？

Would you take students to the library?

どこに音楽室があるか、ご存知ですか？

Do you know where the music room is?

---

2 学校を案内する　　　　　　　　　　Track 148

ここが校長室です。

This is the principal's office.

校長先生がもうすぐ来られます。

Our principal will be here shortly.

単語を覚えましょう

●校内

校長室	principal's room〔office〕
職員室	teachers' room
事務室	secretary's office
放送室	broadcasting room
保健室	nurse's office
1 階	first floor
2 階	second floor
掲示板	notice board

学校生活について話す

1 登校、下校について

【登校】

子供たちはふだん家から小学校まで歩いて登校します。

Children usually go to the elementary school from their homes on foot.

朝、1年生から6年生までのグループが集まります。

A group of first to sixth graders get together in the morning.

交差点で保護者や近所の人たちが子供たちの安全を見守っています。

Parents or neighbors are watching them to be safe at the intersections.

【下校】

放課後、生徒はたいてい歩いて下校します。

After school, students usually walk home.

バスや電車で帰る生徒もいます。

Some students take the bus or train to go home.

2 一日の生活について

【朝の会】

各教室で、担任の先生が生徒の出席や体調をチェックして、その日の予定などを伝えます。

In each classroom, the homeroom teacher checks the attendance and health of the students and tells them the daily information.

【休み時間】

授業と授業の間や給食の後に、休み時間があります。

Between the classes and after school lunch, there are recesses.

外に出てスポーツをする生徒もいれば、教室にいておしゃべりをしたり、本を読む生徒もいます。

Some students go outside and play some sports, others stay in the classrooms to chat or read some books.

【給食】

給食は健康的で栄養バランスが良いです。

School lunch is healthy and well-balanced 〔nutritious〕.

当番の生徒がエプロンと帽子を付けて、各クラスの生徒たちの給食を配膳します。

Duty students wear school aprons and caps to carry and serve their classmates' school lunch in each class.

【掃除】

生徒は給食のあとに教室、廊下や当番の場所を掃除します。

Students clean their classroom, hallway and some duty areas after school lunch.

【部活動】

4年生から、週に1回、クラブ活動があります。

From the fourth grade, they have a club activity once a week.

スポーツや文化クラブから選べます。

There are some sport and culture clubs to choose from.

3 集会について Track 151

【全体集会】

校長先生が体育館の壇上で、1年生から6年生までの生徒の前で話をします。

The school principal speaks on the stage in front of the students from the first (graders) to the sixth graders in the gym.

【学年集会】

同じ学年の先生と生徒が集まって、学校の行事や生活、学習などについて話をします。

Teachers and students in the same grade get together and talk about school events, school life and studies.

4 年間行事について   Track 152

入学式では体育館で校長先生のお話を聞きます。

We will listen to the principal's speech at the entrance ceremony in the gym.

卒業式に出席してもらえますか？

Would you attend the graduation ceremony?

運動会は 10 月に行われます。

The sports day will be held in October.

遠足のおやつは何がいいですか？

What kind of snacks do you want for the field trip?

林間学校に帽子が必要です。

You need your cap for the nature school.

臨海学校はどこに行きますか？

Where are you going on your seaside school?

社会科見学で大阪に行きます。

We will go to Osaka for the social studies trip.

6年生は修学旅行で東京にいます。

Sixth graders are in Tokyo for the school trip.

音楽会で何を演奏しますか？

What will you play for the school's music program?

生徒たちは音楽会で楽器を演奏して、歌を歌います。

The students play some instruments and sing for the school's music program.

生徒たちはとても才能があります。

The students are very talented.

あなたの国で運動会はありますか？

Do you have sports day in your country?

日本の太鼓を見たことはありますか？

Have you seen the Japanese drums?

公開授業のヘルプは必要ですか？

Do you need help for the demonstration class?

単語を覚えましょう

●行事

入学式	entrance ceremony
始業式	opening ceremony
終業式	closing ceremony
卒業式	graduation ceremony
運動会	sports day / field day
音楽会	school's music program
教育実習	practice teaching
公開授業	demonstration class

●校外活動

遠足	field trip / excursion/school picnic
修学旅行	school trip
臨海学校	(summer) seaside school
自然学校	eco-institute
社会科見学	social studies trip
林間学校	nature school / open-air school

●保護者関係の行事

授業参観日	class observation day for parents
家庭訪問	home visit(ing) by teacher
保護者懇談	interview with parents

Part 8

学校生活編

他教科について

1 教科について話す

Track 153

学校でどの教科が好き？

What subject do you like in school?

音楽は好きだけど、算数は好きじゃない。

I like music, but I don't like math.

私は国語が得意だよ。

I'm good at Japanese.

火曜日には国語、算数、体育と社会科があるよ。

We have Japanese, math, P.E. and social studies on Tuesday.

今日、音楽はあった？

Did you have music today?

お習字セットを持って来るのを忘れた。

I forgot to bring the calligraphy set.

今日はテストがあるよ。

We will have a test today.

午後に体育があるよ。

We will have P.E. this afternoon.

理科の先生は理科室にいますか？

Is the science teacher in the science room?

体育の時間は体育館に移動しないといけない。

We have to go to the gym in the P.E. class.

社会科の時間に発表をしないといけない。

You will have a presentation in social studies class.

ミホは習字の大会で賞をもらった。

Miho got a prize in the calligraphy contest.

音楽の授業のためにリコーダーの練習をしないといけない。

I have to practice the recorder for the music class.

漢字の練習が好きじゃない。

I don't like *kanji* practice.

日記を書くのが好きだよ。

I like writing a journal.

単語を覚えましょう

●教室、学習室など

1 年 1 組	First grade class 1
2 年 2 組	Second grade class 2
3 年 3 組	Third grade class 3
4 年 4 組	Fourth grade class 4
理科室	science room
音楽室	music room
図工室	arts and crafts room
調理室	cooking room
家庭科室	sewing room
図書室	library
視聴覚室	audio-visual room
多目的室	multi-purpose room
コンピュータ室	computer room

●校舎外

プール	swimming pool
体育館	gym
運動場	playground
駐車場	parking lot

●共用部分

玄関	entrance hall
生徒用玄関	students' entrance
廊下	hallway
階段	stairs
屋上	rooftop
手洗い場	hand washing area
男子トイレ	boys' toilet
女子トイレ	girls' toilet
職員用トイレ	teachers' toilet

単語を覚えましょう	

●教科

国語	Japanese
算数	math / mathematics
理科	science
社会科	social studies
音楽	music
体育	P.E.
習字	calligraphy
道徳	moral education / ethics
生活	living environmental studies
家庭科	home economics
図画工作	arts and crafts
特別活動	special activities
総合（的な学習の時間）	integrated studies

Part 8

学校生活編

Part 9

いろいろな話題

1 日常の話題

1 日常生活について

【学校、習い事】

生徒は月曜日から金曜日まで学校に行きます。
Students go to school from Monday to Friday.

生徒はたいてい放課後、家に帰ります。
Students usually go home after school.

多くの生徒が放課後に習い事をしています。
Many students go to after school activities.

例えば、スイミングスクール、英語学校、習字、塾などが人気です。
For example, swimming school, English school, calligraphy, cram schools are popular.

【週末、休暇】

週末には、生徒はたいてい家族と一緒に過ごします。
On weekends, students usually spend time with their family.

春休み、ゴールデンウィーク、夏休みや冬休みの間、生徒は家族と一緒に旅行に出かけます。

During spring break, Golden Week, summer break or winter break, students travel with their families.

2 春休み、夏休み、冬休みの予定 Track 155

春休みの予定は？

What's your plan for spring break?

夏休みの予定は？

What's your plan for summer break?

冬休みの予定は？

What's your plan for winter break?

「I will ~」は「私は~します」って意味。

"I will ~" means "*Watashi wa ~ shimasu.*"

例えば、山に行くよ。

For example, I will go to the mountain.

海に行くよ。

I will go to the sea.

ハイキングに行くよ。

I will go hiking.

キャンプに行くよ。

I will go camping.

動物園に行くよ。

I will go to the zoo.

泳ぎに行くよ。

I will go swimming.

魚釣りに行くよ。

I will go fishing.

買い物に行くよ。

I will go shopping.

映画に行くよ。

I will go to the movie.

遊園地に行くよ。

I will go to an amusement park.

祖父母の家に行くよ。

I will go to my grandparents' house.

まだ決まってないけれど、したいことについて話す時は「want to」を使って。

Use "want to" when you talk about something you would like to do even it hasn't been decided yet.

例えば、春休みに遊園地に行きたいよ。

For example, I want to go to an amusement park during spring break.

ジェットコースターに乗りたいよ。

I want to ride a roller coaster.

友だちにおみやげを買いたいよ。

I want to buy some souvenir for my friends.

夏休みに泳ぎに行きたいよ。

I want to go swimming during summer break.

カニをつかまえたいよ。

I want to catch some crabs.

浜辺でアイスクリームを食べたいよ。

I want to eat ice cream at the beach.

冬休みに映画を観に行きたいよ。

I want to go to the movie during winter break.

映画を観たいよ。

I want to watch a movie.

ポップコーンを食べたいよ。

I want to eat some popcorn.

【ゲーム】

私はゲームをするのが大好きです。
I love playing games.

特に好きなものはマインクラフトです。
My favorite one is Minecraft.

レアアイテムを見つけるのが楽しいです。
It is fun to find rare items.

好きなゲームは何ですか？
What is your favorite game?

【TouTube】

毎日 YouTube を観るのを楽しんでいます。
I enjoy watching YouTube every day.

私の好きなチャンネルはアニマル TV です。
My favorite channel is Animal TV.

アニマル TV はとてもおもしろいです。
Animal TV is very funny.

好きな YouTube のチャンネルは何ですか？

What is your favorite YouTube channel?

【アニメ、マンガ】

私は、となりのトトロが好きです。

I like *Tonari no Totoro*.

何度も観ています。

I watched it many times.

私はネコバスが好きです。

I like the Neko-bus.　※ the Cat Bus とも言います。

乗ってみたいです。

I want to ride it.

【音楽】

私はKポップがとても好きです。

I like K-pop very much.

TWICE が私のお気に入りです。

TWICE is my favorite.

TWICE がかわいいです。

TWICE is cute.

コンサートに行きたいです。

I want to go to the concert.

---

4 将来の夢について話す　　　　Track 157

【英語を勉強する】

私は通訳者になりたいです。

I want to be an interpreter.

英語が好きだからです。

Because I like English.

通訳をして、人の役に立ちたいです。

I want to interpret to help people.

だから、一生懸命に英語の勉強をしています。

So, I'm studying English seriously.

【職業】

フライトアテンダント〔客室乗務員〕になりたい。

I want to be a flight attendant.

花屋になりたい。

I want to be a florist.

獣医になりたい。

I want to be a vet.

動物看護士になりたい。

I want to be an animal health technician.

トリマーになりたい。

I want to be a groomer.

犬の訓練士になりたい。

I want to be a dog trainer.

ブリーダーになりたい。

I want to be a breeder.

農場経営者になりたい。

I want to be a farmer.

お笑い芸人になりたい。

I want to be a comedian.

歌手になりたい。

I want to be a singer.

シンガーソングライターになりたい。

I want to be a singer-songwriter.

ユーチューバーになりたい。

I want to be a YouTube personality.

料理人になりたい。

I want to be a cook.

フィギュアスケートの選手になりたい。

I want to be a figure skater.

自衛官になりたい。

I want to be a self-defense official.

養蜂家になりたい。

I want to be a beekeeper.

コーチになりたい。

I want to be a coach.

将棋棋士になりたい。

I want to be a Japanese chess player 〔*Shogi* player〕.

学芸員になりたい。

I want to be a curator.

司書になりたい。

I want to be a librarian.

登山家になりたい。

I want to be a mountain climber.

エンジニアになりたい。

I want to be an engineer.

カメラマンになりたい。

I want to be a photographer.

カーレーサーになりたい。

I want to be a car racer.

ツアーコンダクターになりたい。

I want to be a tour conductor.

日本語教師になりたい。

I want to be a Japanese language teacher.

翻訳家になりたい。

I want to be a translator.

テレビディレクターになりたい。

I want to be a TV director.

映画監督になりたい。

I want to be a movie director.

測量士になりたい。

I want to be a land surveyor.

精神科医になりたい。

I want to be a psychiatrist.

臨床心理士になりたい。

I want to be a clinical psychotherapist.

大工になりたい。

I want to be a carpenter.

インテリアコーディネーターになりたい。

I want to be an Interior coordinator.

不動産屋になりたい。

I want to be a real estate agent.

ファッションデザイナーになりたい。

I want to be a fashion designer.

ジュエリーデザイナーになりたい。

I want to be a jewelry designer.

ファッションモデルになりたい。

I want to be a fashion model.

アナウンサーになりたい。

I want to be an announcer.

単語を覚えましょう

●職業

アナウンサー	announcer	学芸員	curator
エンジニア	engineer	通訳者	interpreter
モデル	model	翻訳家	translator
料理人	cook	登山家	climber
花屋	florist	獣医	vet
映画監督	movie director	大工	carpenter

2 様々なトピック

1 世界の国々について

世界には190以上の国があります。

There are more than 190 countries around the globe.

いくつの国を知っていますか？

How many countries do you know?

日本のパスポートを持っていれば、ほとんどの国を訪れることができます。

If we have a Japanese passport, we can visit most of them.

どの国に行ってみたいですか？

What country do you want to visit?

私はタイに行ってみたいです。

I want to visit Thailand.

理由は大きな象に乗ってみたいからです。

Because I want to ride a big elephant.

タイの伝統的な衣装を着てみたいです。

I want to wear traditional Thai clothing.

タイ料理を食べてみたいです。

I want to eat Thai food.

2 行ってみたい国について

イタリアに行ってみたい。

I want to go to Italy.

（イタリアは）ヨーロッパにあるよ。

It's in Europe.

人々はイタリア語を話すよ。

They speak Italian.

ローマはイタリアの首都だよ。

Rome is the capital of Italy.

ピザとパスタがイタリアでは人気だよ。

Pizza and pasta are popular in Italy.

アメリカに行ってみたい。

I want to go to America.

（アメリカは）北アメリカ大陸にあるよ。

It's on the North American continent.

人々は英語とスペイン語を話すよ。

They speak English and Spanish.

ワシントン D.C. がアメリカの首都だよ。

Washington D.C. is the capital of (the United States of) America.

ハンバーガーとアップルパイがアメリカでは人気だよ。

Hamburgers and apple pies are popular in America.

カナダに行ってみたい。

I want to go to Canada.

（カナダは）北アメリカ大陸にあるよ。

It's on the North American continent.

人々は英語とフランス語を話すよ。

They speak English and French.

オタワはカナダの首都だよ。

Ottawa is the capital of Canada.

メープルシロップとチキンウィングがカナダでは人気だよ。

Maple syrup and chicken wings are popular in Canada.

オーストラリアに行ってみたい。

I want to go to Australia.

（オーストラリアは）南半球にあるよ。

It's in the south Hemisphere.

人々は英語を話すよ。

They speak English.

キャンベラはオーストラリアの首都だよ。

Canberra is the capital of Australia.

ミートパイとマッシュポテトがオーストラリアでは人気だよ。

Meat Pie and Mashed Potato are popular in Australia.

3 日本について　　　　　　　　　　　　　　Track 160

【日本の文化】

私は日本の文化が好きです。

I like Japanese culture.

特に、日本食と着物が好きです。

Especially, Japanese food and *kimono*.

日本食は健康的だし、着物は美しいです。

Japanese food is healthy, and *kimono* is beautiful.

あなたは日本の文化に興味はありますか？

Are you interested in Japanese culture?

【日本の観光名所】

東京に行きました。
I went to Tokyo.

東京スカイツリーは日本で一番高い塔です。
Tokyo Sky Tree is the highest tower in Japan.

壮大な景色が見られます。
It has a splendid view.

ぜひ東京スカイツリーに行ってください。
You should visit Tokyo Sky Tree.

4 スポーツ大会について　　　　　Track 161

私はテニスの試合が観たいです。
I want to watch tennis matches.

テニスをしているからです。
Because I play tennis.

あなたは何を観戦したいですか？
What do you want to watch?

バスケを見たいよ。

I want to watch basketball.

野球を見たいよ。

I want to watch baseball.

セーリングを見たいよ。

I want to watch sailing.

車いすテニスを見たいよ。

I want to watch wheelchair tennis.

陸上を見たいよ。

I want to watch athletics.

空手を見たいよ。

I want to watch _karate_.

バドミントンを見たいよ。

I want to watch badminton.

ソフトボールを見たいよ。

I want to watch softball.

オリンピック中に何を見たいかな？

What do you want to watch during the Olympics?

開会式を見たいよ。

I want to watch the opening ceremony.

ボクシングを見たいよ。

I want to watch boxing.

カヌーを見たいよ。

I want to watch canoe.

サーフィンを見たいよ。

I want to watch surfing.

卓球を見たいよ。

I want to watch table tennis.

テコンドーを見たいよ。

I want to watch taekwondo.

テニスを見たいよ。

I want to watch tennis.

トライアスロンを見たいよ。

I want to watch the triathlon.

バレーボールを見たいよ。

I want to watch volleyball.

ウェイトリフティングを見たいよ。

I want to watch weightlifting.

レスリングを見たいよ。

I want to watch wrestling.

5 国際理解について   Track 162

私には韓国人の友だちがいます。

I have a Korean friend.

まったく同じ考えを持っているわけではないけれど、私は友だちのことが
とても好きです。

**We don't have exactly the same ideas, but I like her very
much.**

その子の考えを知るのはすばらしいです。

It is nice to know her thoughts.

国際的な友だちっていますか？

Do you have any international friends?

6 和製英語について   Track 163

和製英語って知っていますか？

Do you know *Wasei* English?

英語のように使われていると信じている人もいます。

We sometimes believe they are used like English.

でも誤解させることもよくあります。

But they sometimes confuse people.

だから、違いを理解するべきです。

So, we should know the differences.

---

7 環境問題について　　　　　　　　　Track 164

たくさんのゴミを食べたために死んだクジラを見ました。

I saw a whale that died because it ate a lot of garbage.

私は悲しくて、泣きました。

I was sad, and I cried.

私たちは川や海をきれいにするべきだと思います。

We should clean the rivers and oceans.

あなたはどう思いますか？

What do you think?

単語を覚えましょう

●自然

山	mountain	陸	land
森	forest	野原	field
海	ocean/sea	丘	hill
川	river	湖	lake

●四季

| 春 | spring | 秋 | autumn/fall |
| 夏 | summer | 冬 | winter |

＜参考＞

※英検 Jr.、英検 5 級、英検 4 級を受ける時の練習に
　使えるフレーズを掲載しています。
　（音声は録音されていません）

英検 Jr.（Bronze/Silver/Gold）

<各級のテストを始めるまでの準備>

英検 Jr. ブロンズレベルの練習をしましょう。

Let's practice Eiken Jr. Bronze level.

英検 Jr. シルバーレベルの練習をしましょう。

Let's practice Eiken Jr. Silver level.

英検 Jr. ゴールドレベルの練習をしましょう。

Let's practice Eiken Jr. Gold level.

これはテストではありません。

This is not a test.

簡単なリスニングクイズです。

It's an easy listening quiz.

これを見て。

Look at this.

この冊子を見て。

Look at this brochure.

表紙に、名前を書いて。

On the front page, write your name.

まず、ひらがなで。

First, in *hiragana*.

名字と名前を分けてね。

Your family name and first name separately.

次に、誕生日を書いてね。
Next, write your birthday.

月と日ね。
Month and date.

学年とクラスね。
Your grade and class.

アルファベットで名前を書いてね。
Write your name using the alphabet.

また、名字と名前を分けてね。
Separate your family name and first name, again.

年齢を書いて。
Write your age.

学年を選んで、数字のところに○を書いて。
Choose your grade and write a circle around the number.

性別、男性か女性かを選んでね。
Choose your gender, male(boy) or female(girl).

どれくらいの間、英語の勉強をしている？
How long have you been studying English?

英検の級を持っている？
Do you have an Eiken grade(score)?

もし英検を受けたことがなかったら、1を選んでね。
If you haven't taken the Eiken, please choose 1.

もし英検のことを知らなかったら、1を選んでね。

If you don't know of the Eiken, please choose 1.

全部記入した？

Did you fill out everything?

何か質問があれば、手を挙げてね。

If you have any questions, please raise your hand.

最初のページを開いて、左側を見て。

Open the first page, and look at the left side.

これが◯の描き方だよ。

This is how you draw a circle.

◆英検 Jr.（Bronze）の内容を説明する

①

1ページを見て。

Look at page 1.

8つの絵があるね。

There are eight pictures.

それらをよく見てね。

Look at them carefully.

1分あげるね。

I'll give you one minute.

では、CD を聞いてね。

Now, listen to the CD.

3つの文が聞こえてくるよ。

You'll listen to three sentences.

正しいものを選んで、四角に○を書いてね。

Choose the correct one and write a circle in the box.

一緒に最初の問題をします。

We will try the first question together.

一緒に答えを確認しよう。

Let's check the answer together.

どれを選んだ？

Which one did you choose?

正解は 1。

The correct answer is 1.

赤エンピツか赤ペンを使って答えをチェックしてね。

Use your red pencil or red pen to check your answer.

次の問題へ行くよ。

Let's move on to the next question.

2から8まで。

From 2 to 8.

8つの問題が終わったら、一緒に答えをチェックするよ。

When you finish eight questions, check your answers together.

がんばったね。

Well done.

---

②

2ページを見て。

Look at page 2.

Yes, (or) No クイズだよ。

Yes, or No quiz.

最初の絵を見て。

Look at the first picture.

絵の中の人が質問をするよ。

Person in the picture will ask a question.

そして3つの返事が聞こえるよ。

And you will hear three answers.

3つの中から正しい答えを選んで。

Choose the correct answer of the three.

一緒に最初の問題をします。

We will try the first question together.

一緒に答えを確認しよう。

Let's check the answer together.

どれを選んだ？

Which one did you choose?

正解は2。

The correct answer is 2.

9から13までやろうね。

Let's move on to 9 to 13.

5つの問題が終わったら、一緒に答えをチェックしよう。

When you finish five questions, check your answers together.

③

3ページを見て。

Look at page 3.

スリーヒントクイズだよ。

This is a three hint quiz.

6枚の絵を見てね。

Look at the six pictures.

彼らはそれぞれ何か違うことをしているよね。

They are each doing something different.

色を見て。

Look at the colors.

彼らが持っているものを見て。

Look what they have.

彼らの顔を見て。

Look at their faces.

1分あげるね。

I'll give you one minute.

では、CDを聞いてね。

Now, listen to the CD.

正しい答えを選んで、四角に○を書いてね。

Choose the correct answer and write a circle in the box.

間違ったものを選ばないように、よく聞いてね。

You have to listen carefully not to choose the wrong one.

一緒に最初の問題をします。

We will try the first question together.

一緒に答えを確認しよう。

Let's check the answer together.

どれを選んだ？

Which one did you choose?

正解は 1。

The correct answer is 1.

14 から 17 までやろうね。

Let's move on to 14 to 17.

4 つの問題が終わったら、一緒に答えをチェックしよう。

When you finish four questions, check your answer together.

がんばったね。

Well done.

④

4 ページを見て。

Look at page 4.

ナレーションを聞いて、正しい絵を選んでね。

Listen to the narration and choose the correct picture.

文章を2回聞けるよ。

You can listen to the sentences twice.

各問題の3枚の絵を見てね。

Look at the three pictures in each question.

違いは何かな？／どう違うかな？

What are the differences? / How are they different?

1分あげるね。

I'll give you one minute.

CDを聞いてね。

Listen to the CD.

正しい答えを選んで、四角に○を書いてね。

Choose the correct answer and write a circle in the box.

一緒に最初の問題をします。

We will try the first question together.

一緒に答えを確認しよう。

Let's check the answer together.

どれを選んだ？

Which one did you choose?

正解は3。

The correct answer is 3.

19から21までやろうね。

Let's move on to 19 to 21.

22 から 25 は別のお話だよ。

There is another narration from 22 to 25.

全部終わったら、一緒に答え合わせをしようね。

When you finish all of them, let's check your answers together.

がんばったね。

Well done.

⑤

6ページを見て。

Look at page 6.

会話を聞いて、正しい絵を選んでね。

Listen to the conversation and choose the correct picture.

文章を 2 回聞けるよ。

You can listen to the sentences twice.

4枚の絵を見て。

Look at the four pictures.

彼らは何をしているかな？

What are they doing?

1分あげるね。

I'll give you one minute.

CD を聞いてね。

Listen to the CD.

正しい絵を選んで、四角に○を書いてね。

Choose the correct picture and write a circle in the box.

一緒に最初の問題をするね。

We will try the first question together.

一緒に答えを確認しよう。

Let's check the answer together.

どれを選んだ？

Which one did you choose?

正解は 2。

The correct answer is 2.

27 から 28 をやろうね。

Let's move on to 27 to 28.

29 から 31 は別の会話だよ。

There is another conversation from 29 to 31.

全部の問題が終わったら、一緒に答えをチェックしよう。

When you finish all the questions, check your answers together.

がんばったね。

Well done.

⑥

8 ページを見て。

Look at page 8.

4 人の子どもがいるよ。

There are four children.

それぞれが違う質問をされて、答えているよ。

They are asked different questions, and they answer.

それぞれの子どもは2つか3つの答えを言っているよ。

Each child says two or three answers.

一緒に最初の問題をやってみよう。

We will try the first question together.

質問は「彼らは何を持っているの？」だよ。

The question is, "What do they have?"

33から35をやろうね。

Let's move on to 33 to 35.

文章を2回聞けるよ。

You can listen to the sentences twice.

では、CDを聞いてね。

Now, listen to the CD.

全部の問題が終わったら、一緒に答えをチェックしよう。

When you finish all the questions, check your answers together.

がんばったね。

Well done.

⑦

9ページを見て。

Look at page 9.

文章を2回聞けるよ。

You can listen to the sentences twice.

では、CD を聞いてね。

Now, listen to the CD.

正しい答えを選んで、四角に○を書いてね。

Choose the correct answer and write a circle in the box.

一緒に最初の問題をやってみよう。

We will try the first question together.

一緒に答えを確認しよう。

Let's check the answer together.

どれを選んだ？

Which one did you choose?

正解は1。

The correct answer is 1.

37 から 40 までやろうね。

Let's move on to 37 to 40.

チャレンジコーナー

10 ページを見て。

Look at page 10.

次は最後の問題で、「チャレンジコーナー」だよ。
これは合計ポイントに含まれません。
それで、「Yes」または「Good」と思ったら、1 を選んでね。
「No」または「Not good」と思ったら、2 を選んで。

The next one is the last section, "Challenge corner."
This is not included in the total points.
So, if you believe it is 'Yes' or 'Good', choose one.
If you think 'No' or 'Not good', choose two.

文章を 2 回聞けるよ。

You can listen to the sentences twice.

みんな、がんばったね。

Well done, everybody.

これで終わりです。

This is the end.

◆英検 Jr.（Silver）の内容を説明する

①

1 ページを見て。

Look at page 1.

8 つの絵があるね。

There are eight pictures.

それらをよく見てね。

Look at them carefully.

1 分あげるね。

I'll give you one minute.

では、CD を聞いてね。

Now, listen to the CD.

3つの文が聞こえてくるよ。

You'll listen to three sentences.

正しい答えを選んで、四角に○を書いてね。

Choose the correct one and write a circle in the box.

一緒に最初の問題をするよ。

We will try the first question together.

一緒に答えを確認しよう。

Let's check the answer together.

どれを選んだ？

Which one did you choose?

正解は1。

The correct answer is 1.

赤エンピツか赤ペンを使って答えをチェックしてね。

Use your red pencil or red pen to check your answer.

次の問題へ行くよ。

Let's move on to the next question.

2から8まで。

From 2 to 8.

全部終わったら、一緒に答えをチェックするよ。

When you finish all of them, let's check your answers together.

がんばったね。

Well done.

2ページを見て。

Look at page 2.

最初の絵を見てね。

Look at the first picture.

(　　　　) が質問をするよ。

(　　　　) **will ask a question.**

そして、2つの返事が聞こえるよ。

And you will hear two answers.

2つの中から正しい答えを選んでね。

Choose the correct answer from the two.

一緒に最初の問題をします。

We will try the first question together.

一緒に答えを確認しよう。

Let's check the answer together.

どれを選んだ？

Which one did you choose?

正解は〜。

The correct answer is ~.

10から12までやろうね。

Let's move on to 10 to 12.

全部終わったら、一緒に答えをチェックしよう。

When you finish them, check your answers together.

③

3ページを見て。

Look at page 3.

CD を聞いてね。

Listen to the CD.

（同じ種類の）4つの単語が聞こえるよ。

You will hear four words (in the same category).

同じものを絵の中で見つけて、番号を選んでね。

Find the same things in the picture and choose the numbers.

聞こえたものが絵の中に見つからない場合もあるよ。

You may not find everything you hear in the picture.

13番の問題をやってみよう。

Try question number 13.

次の問題へ行くよ。

Let's move on to the next question.

それらが終わったら、一緒に答えをチェックしよう。

When you finish them, check your answers together.

がんばったね。

Well done.

④

4ページを見て。

Look at page 4.

スリーヒントクイズだよ。

This is a three hint quiz.

6 枚の絵を見て。

Look at the six pictures.

彼らは何か違うことをしているね。

They are each doing something different.

色を見て。

Look at the colors.

彼らが持っているものを見て。

Look what they have.

彼らの顔を見て。

Look at their faces.

1 分あげるね。

I'll give you one minute.

では、CD を聞いてね。

Now, listen to the CD.

正しい答えを選んで、四角に○を書いてね。

Choose the correct answer and write a circle in the box.

間違ったものを選ばないように、よく聞かなければいけないよ。

You have to listen carefully not to choose the wrong one.

一緒に最初の問題をしよう。

We will try the first question together.

一緒に答えを確認しよう。

Let's check the answer together.

どれを選んだ？

Which one did you choose?

正解は 1。

The correct answer is 1.

17 から 19 をやろうね。

Let's move on to 17 to 19.

それらが終わったら、一緒に答えをチェックしよう。

When you finish them, check your answers together.

がんばったね。

Well done.

⑤

5 ページを見てね。

Look at page 5.

CD を聞いて、3 つの単語を聞いてね。

Listen to the CD and hear three words.

それらは同じ音のアルファベットで始まるよ。

They start from the same sound of the alphabet.

単語を 1 回聞けるよ。

You can listen to the words once.

20番の問題をやってみよう。

Let's try question number 20.

正しい答えは～。

The correct answer is ~.

正しいアルファベットは～。

The correct letter is ~.

21から23をやろうね。

Let's move on to 21 to 23.

それらが終わったら、一緒に答えをチェックしよう。

When you finish them, check your answers together.

みんな、がんばったね。

Well done, everybody.

⑥

6ページを見てね。

Look at page 6.

2枚の絵を見てね。

Look at the two pictures.

違いは何かな？／どう違うかな？

What are the differences? / How are they different?

1分あげるね。

I'll give you one minute.

では、CD を聞いてね。

Now, listen to the CD.

正しい絵を選んで、四角に○を書いてね。

Choose the correct picture and write a circle in the box.

一緒に最初の問題をやってみよう。

We will try the first question together.

一緒に答えを確認しよう。

Let's check the answer together.

どちらを選んだ？

Which one did you choose?

正解は〜。

The correct answer is ~.

25 から 27 をやろうね。

Let's move on to 25 to 27.

それらが終わったら、一緒に答えをチェックしよう。

When you finish them, let's check your answers together.

7 ページを見てね。

Look at page 7.

前の問題と同じパターンだね。

It is the same pattern as the previous one.

それらが終わったら、一緒に答えをチェックしよう。

When you finish them, let's check your answer together.

がんばったね。

Well done.

---

⑦

8ページを見てね。

Look at page 8.

各問題の3枚の絵を見てね。

Look at the three pictures in each question.

違いは何かな？／どう違うかな？

What are the differences? / How are they different?

1分あげるね。

I'll give you one minute.

では、CDを聞いてね。

Now, listen to the CD.

正しい答えを選んで、四角に○を書いてね。

Choose the correct answer and write a circle in the box.

一緒に最初の問題をします。

We will try the first question together.

文章を2回聞けるよ。

You can listen to the sentences twice.

では、CDを聞いてね。

Now, listen to the CD.

正しい答えを選んで、四角に○を書いてね。
Choose the correct answer and write a circle in the box.

一緒に最初の問題をします。
We will try the first question together.

一緒に答えを確認しよう。
Let's check the answer together.

どれを選んだ？
Which one did you choose?

正解は〜。
The correct answer is ~.

33 から 37 までやろうね。
Let's move on to 33 to 37.

それらが終わったら、一緒に答えをチェックしよう。
When you finish them, let's check your answers together.

がんばったね。
Well done.

⑧

10 ページを見てね。
Look at page 10.

絵を見てね。
Look at the picture.

～が…について２人に聞くよ。

～ ask two people about ….

会話を聞いて、正しい絵を選んでね。

Listen to the conversation and choose the correct picture.

会話を２回聞けるよ。

You can listen to the conversation twice.

正しい答えを選んで、四角に○を書いてね。

Choose the correct answer and write a circle in the box.

一緒に最初の問題をします。

We will try the first question together.

一緒に答えを確認しよう。

Let's check the answer together.

どれを選んだ？

Which one did you choose?

正解は～。

The correct answer is ~.

39 をやろうね。

Let's move on to 39.

今度は２つの答えを選んでね。

You have to choose two answers this time.

それらが終わったら、一緒に答えをチェックしよう。

When you finish them, let's check your answers together.

みんな、がんばったね。
Well done, everybody.

---

⑨

13ページを見てね。
Look at page 13.

絵を見てね。
Look at the pictures.

単語もありますね。
You'll see the words too.

単語を聞いて、正しい番号を選んでね。
Listen to the word and choose the correct number.

文章を2回聞けるよ。
You can listen to the sentences twice.

1分あげるね。
I'll give you one minute.

では、CDを聞いてね。
Now, listen to the CD.

正しい答えを選んで、四角に○を書いてね。
Choose the correct answer and write a circle in the box.

一緒に最初の問題をやってみよう。
We will try the first question together.

一緒に答えを確認しよう。

Let's check the answer together.

どれを選んだ？

Which one did you choose?

正解は〜。

The correct answer is ~.

43 から 45 をやろうね。

Let's move on to 43 to 45.

それらが終わったら、一緒に答えをチェックしよう。

When you finish them, check your answers together.

がんばったね。

Well done.

チャレンジコーナー

---

14 ページを見て。

Look at page 14.

次は最後のセクションで、「チャレンジコーナー」だよ。
これは合計ポイントに含まれません。
それで、「Yes」または「Good」と思ったら、1 を選んでね。
「No」または「Not good」と思ったら、2 を選んでね。

The next one is the last section,"Challenge corner."
This is not included in the total points.
So, if you believe it is 'Yes' or 'Good', choose one.
If you think 'No' or 'Not good', choose two.

文章をもう一度、聞けるよ。

You can listen to the sentences once.

みんな、がんばったね。

Well done, everybody.

これで終わりです。

This is the end.

◆英検 Jr.（Gold）の内容を説明する

①

1ページを見て。

Look at page 1.

8つの絵があるね。

There are eight pictures.

それらをよく見てね。

Look at them carefully.

1分あげるね。

I'll give you one minute.

では、CD を聞いてね。

Now, listen to the CD.

3つの文が聞こえてくるよ。

You'll listen to three sentences.

正しい答えを選んで、四角に○を書いてね。

Choose the correct one and write a circle in the box.

一緒に最初の問題をするよ。

We will try the first question together.

一緒に答えを確認しよう。

Let's check the answer together.

どれを選んだ？

Which one did you choose?

正解は1。

The correct answer is 1.

赤エンピツか赤ペンを使って答えをチェックしてね。

Use your red pencil or red pen to check your answer.

次の問題へ行きましょう。

Let's move on to the next question.

2から8まで。

From 2 to 8.

全部終わったら、一緒に答えをチェックしよう。

When you finish all of them, let's check your answers together.

がんばったね。

Well done.

---

②

2ページを見てね。

Look at page 2.

絵はありません。

There is no picture.

CD をよく聞いてね。

Listen to the CD carefully.

4 つの単語が聞こえるよ。

You'll hear four words.

同じグループに属さないものを 1 つ選んでね。

Choose one word which doesn't belong to the same group.

同じカテゴリーに属さないものを 1 つ選んでね。

Choose one word which doesn't belong to the same category.

四角に◯を描いてね。

Draw a circle in the box.

一緒に最初の問題をするよ。

We will try the first question together.

一緒に答えを確認しよう。

Let's check the answer together.

どれを選んだ？

Which one did you choose?

正解は〜。

The correct answer is ~.

次の問題へ行きましょう。

Let's move on to the next questions.

10 から 14 まで。

From 10 to 14.

全部終わったら、一緒に答えをチェックしよう。

When you finish all of them, let's check your answers together.

みんな、がんばったね。

Well done, everybody.

③

3ページを見てね。

Look at page 3.

8つの絵があるね。

There are eight pictures.

それらをよく見てね。

Look at them carefully.

1分あげるね。

I'll give you one minute.

では、CDを聞いてね。

Now, listen to the CD.

最初の絵を見てね。

Look at the first picture.

会話を聞いて、正しい答えを選んでね。

You'll hear a conversation and choose the correct answer.

2つの中から正しい答えを選んでね。

Choose the correct answer from the two.

一緒に最初の問題をします。

We will try the first question together.

一緒に答えを確認しよう。

Let's check the answer together.

どちらを選んだ？

Which one did you choose?

正解は〜。

The correct answer is ~.

16 から 20 までやろうね。

Let's move on to 16 to 20.

それらが終わったら、一緒に答えをチェックしよう。

When you finish them, let's check your answers together.

がんばったね。

Well done.

4 ページを見てね。

Look at page 4.

6 枚の絵を見てね。

Look at the six pictures.

1 分あげるね。

I'll give you one minute.

ナレーションを聞いて、正しい絵を選んでね。

Listen to the narration and choose the correct picture.

ナレーションを1回だけ聞けるよ。

You can hear the narration only once.

では、CD を聞いてね。

Now, listen to the CD.

正しい答えを選んで、四角に○を書いてね。

Choose the correct answer and write a circle in the box.

一緒に最初の問題をします。

We will try the first question together.

一緒に答えを確認しようね。

Let's check the answer together.

どれを選んだ？

Which one did you choose?

正解は～。

The correct answer is ~.

22 から 25 までやろうね。

Let's move on to 22 to 25.

全部終わったら、一緒に答えをチェックしよう。

When you finish all of them, let's check your answers together.

がんばったね。

Well done.

⑤

6ページと7ページを見てね。

Look at page 6 and 7.

7枚の絵を見て。

Look at the seven pictures.

番号の隣の単語を読めたら、正しい答えを選べるよ。

If you can read the word next to the number, you can choose the correct answer.

1分あげるね。

I'll give you one minute.

正しい答えを選んで、四角に○を書いてね。

Choose the correct answer and write a circle in the box.

一緒に最初の問題をしようね。

We will try the first question together.

実は、音が聞こえるだけだよ。

Actually, you only hear a tone.

一緒に答えを確認しようね。

Let's check the answer together.

どれを選んだ？

Which one did you choose?

正解は〜。

The correct answer is ~.

27 から 31 までやろうね。

Let's move on to 27 to 31.

全部終わったら、一緒に答えをチェックしよう。

When you finish all of them, let's check your answers together.

がんばったね。

Well done.

⑥

8 ページを見てね。

Look at page 8.

絵があります。

There is a picture.

1 分あげるね。

I'll give you one minute.

1 つの質問と 2 つの答えが聞こえるよ。

You'll hear a question and two answers.

2 回聞けるよ。

You can listen to it twice.

では、CD を聞いてね。

Now listen to the CD.

正しい答えを選んで、四角に○を書いてね。

Choose the correct answer and write a circle in the box.

一緒に最初の問題をします。

We will try the first question together.

一緒に答えを確認しようね。

Let's check the answer together.

どちらを選んだ？

Which one did you choose?

正解は～。

The correct answer is ~.

33 から 35 までやろうね。

Let's move on to 33 to 35.

全部終わったら、一緒に答えをチェックしよう。

When you finish all of them, let's check your answers together.

9 ページを見てね。

Look at page 9.

もう 1 枚の絵があるよ。

There is another picture.

同じパターンだから、36 から 39 までやってみよう。

It is the same pattern, so try 36 to 39.

全部終わったら、一緒に答えをチェックしよう。

When you finish all of them, let's check your answers together.

がんばったね。

Well done.

10 ページを見て。

Look at page 10.

絵を見て。

Look at the picture.

2 人の会話を聞いた後、3 つの文が聞こえます。

After a conversation between two people, you'll hear three sentences.

どれが正しいでしょう？

Which statement is correct?

文章を 2 回聞けるよ。

You can listen to the sentences twice.

では、CD を聞いてね。

Now, listen to the CD.

正しい答えを選んで、四角に○を書いてね。

Choose the correct answer and write a circle in the box.

一緒に最初の問題をします。

We will try the first question together.

一緒に答えを確認しよう。

Let's check the answer together.

どれを選んだ？

Which one did you choose?

正解は〜。

The correct answer is ~.

41 と 42 をやろうね。

Let's move on to 41 to 42.

全部終わったら、一緒に答えをチェックしよう。

When you finish all of them, let's check your answer together.

がんばったね。

Well done.

⑧

11 ページを見てね。

Look at page 11.

絵を見てね。

Look at the picture.

何人かいるね。

There are some people.

説明と英文を聞いた後、3つの中から一番適切な質問を選んでね。

After the explanation and an English sentence, choose the best question you should ask from the three.

文章を2回聞けるよ。

You can listen to the sentences twice.

では、CD を聞いてね。

Now, listen to the CD.

正しい答えを選んで、四角に○を書いてね。

Choose the correct answer and write a circle in the box.

一緒に最初の問題をします。

We will try the first question together.

一緒に答えを確認しよう。

Let's check the answer together.

どれを選んだ？

Which one did you choose?

正解は〜。

The correct answer is ~.

44 から 46 をやろうね。

Let's move on to 44 to 46.

全部終わったら、一緒に答えをチェックしよう。

When you finish all of them, let's check your answer together.

がんばったね。

Well done.

⑨

4 コマ漫画を見てね。

Look at four-frame cartoon.

2 番目と 4 番目の絵の中で、せりふが抜けているよ。

In the second and fourth frames, dialogues are missing.

それぞれ最も良いと思うせりふを選んでね。

Choose the best dialogue for each.

文章を2回聞けるよ。

You can listen to the sentences twice.

では、CDを聞いてね。

Now, listen to the CD.

正しい答えを選んで、四角に○を書いてね。

Choose the correct answer and write a circle in the box.

一緒に最初の問題をします。

We will try the first question together.

一緒に答えを確認しよう。

Let's check the answer together.

どれを選んだ？

Which one did you choose?

正解は～。

The correct answer is ~.

48から50をやろうね。

Let's move on to 48 to 50.

全部終わったら、一緒に答えを確認しよう。

When you finish all of them, let's check your answer together.

がんばったね。

Well done.

14 ページを見て。

Look at page 14.

次は最後のセクションで、「チャレンジコーナー」だよ。
これは合計ポイントに含まれません。
それで、「Yes」または「Good」と思ったら、1を選んでね。
「No」または「Not good」と思ったら、2を選んでね。

The next one is the last section,"Challenge corner."
This is not included in the total points.
So, if you believe it is 'Yes' or 'Good', choose one.
If you think 'No' or 'Not good', choose two.

文章をもう一度聞けるよ。

You can listen to the sentences once.

みんな、がんばったね。

Well done, everybody.

これで終わりです。

This is the end.

英検 5 級の内容を説明する

英検5級の練習をしましょう。

Let's practice Eiken grade 5.

リーディングには3つのセクションがあります。

There are three sections in reading.

リスニングも3つのセクションがあります。

There are three sections in listening, too.

リーディング

リーディングのセクション 1 には、15問あります。

In reading section 1, there are 15 questions.

各問題に、4つの選択肢があります。

In each question, there are four choices.

正しいと思う選択肢を選んでね。

Choose the best choice you think it is correct.

一緒に 1 番をやってみよう。

Let's try No.1 together.

空欄に最も適した選択肢はどれと思う？

Which do you think is the best choice for the blank?

1分あげるね。

I'll give you 1 minute.

正しい答えは3です。

The correct answer is 3.

問題 2 番から 15 番をやってみよう。

Try question No.2 to 15.

10分あげるね。

I'll give you 10 minutes.

答えを確認しましょう、そして説明するね。

Let's check your answers and let me explain.

セクション 2 には、5問あるよ。

In section 2, there are 5 questions.

問題 16 番を見て。

Look at question No.16.

2 人の会話だよ。

This is a conversation between two people.

誰が話しているか、わかる？

Do you know who is talking?

2 人目は何と答えたかな？

What did the second person answer?

選択肢は 4 つあるよ。

There are four choices.

正しいと思う選択肢を選んでね。

Choose the best choice you think it is correct.

10 秒あげるね。

I'll give you 10 seconds.

一緒に問題 16 番をやってみよう。

Let's try question No.16 together.

正しいと思う選択肢を選んでね。

Choose the best choice you think it is correct.

10 秒あげるね。

I'll give you 10 seconds.

正しい答えは 2 です。

The correct answer is 2.

問題 17 番から 20 番をやってみて。

Try question No.17 to 20.

4 分あげるね。

I'll give you 4 minutes.

答えを確認しましょう。

Let's check your answers.

セクション 3 には、5 問あるよ。

In section 3, there are 5 questions.

21 番を読んでね。

Read No.21.

まず、しっかりと日本語の文を読んでね。

First, read the Japanese sentence carefully.

ホワイトボードを見てね。

Look at the whiteboard.

4 つの単語があるね。

There are four words.

そして 4 つの単語を見て。

And look at the four words.

これらの単語をそれぞれの□に入れてみて。

Put these words into each box.

1 分あげるね。

I'll give you 1 minute.

誰かやってくれる人？

Any volunteers?

答えを確認させて。

Let me check your answer.

それが正しいです。

That's correct.

よくできました！

Good job!

では、最初の□と3番目の□を見て。

Now, look at the first box and the third box.

最初の□は③、3番目の□は②です。

The first box is ③, and the third box is ②.

4つの選択肢を見て。

Look at the four choices.

そう。2だね。

Yes. That's 2.

問題22番から25番をやってみよう。

Try question No.22 to 25.

4分あげるね。

I'll give you 4 minutes.

答えを確認しましょう。

Let's check your answers.

リスニング

リスニングのセクション1には、10問あります。

In listening section 1, there are 10 questions.

10枚の絵があるね。

There are ten pictures.

まず、1番を見て。

First, look at No.1.

CDを聞いて。

Listen to the CD.

2回聞けるよ。

You can listen to it twice.

何番を選んだ？

What number did you choose?

3番が正解だよ。

No.3 is the correct answer.

説明させて。

Let me explain.

では、問題2番から10番をやってみよう。

Now, try question No.2 to 10.

〔10番が終わった後〕
赤ペンか赤エンピツを持っている？

Do you have a red pen or a red pencil?

答えを確認しましょう。

Let's check your answers.

セクション2には、5問あるよ。

In section 2, there are 5 questions.

このセクションに、絵はないよ。

In this section, there are no pictures.

選択肢を読まなければなりません。

You have to read the choices.

それらを声に出して読んで。

Read them out loud.

選択肢1を読んで。

Read the choice 1.

選択肢2を読んで。

Read the choice 2.

選択肢3を読んで。

Read the choice 3.

選択肢4を読んで。

Read the choice 4.

では、CDを聞いて。

Now, listen to the CD.

何番を選んだ？

What number did you choose?

3番が正解だよ。

No.3 is the correct answer.

説明させてね。

Let me explain.

次の問題に進みましょう。

Let's move on to the next questions.

問題 12 番から 15 番をやってみよう。

Try question No.12 to 15.

答えを確認しましょう。

Let's check your answers.

セクション 3 には、10 問あるよ。

In section 3, there are 10 questions.

10 枚の絵があります。

There are ten pictures.

まず、16 番を見て。

First, look at No.16.

CD を聞いて。

Listen to the CD.

2 回聞けるよ。

You can listen to it twice.

選択肢は 3 つあります。

There are three choices.

何番を選んだ？

What number did you choose?

3 番が正解だよ。

No. 3 is the correct answer.

選択肢があるね。

Here are the choices.

次の問題に進みましょう。

Let's move on to the next question.

問題 17 番から 25 番をやってみよう。

Try question No.17 to 25.

答えを確認しましょう。

Let's check your answers.

これでテストは終わりです。

This is the end of the test.

英検 4 級の内容を説明する

英検 4 級の練習をしましょう。

Let's practice Eiken grade 4.

リーディングには 4 つのセクションがあります。

There are four sections in reading.

リスニングには 3 つのセクションがあります。

There are three sections in listening.

リーディング

リーディングのセクション1には、15問あります。
In reading section 1, there are 15 questions.

各問題に、4つの選択肢があります。
In each question, there are four choices.

正しいと思う選択肢を選んでね。
Choose the best choice you think it is correct.

一緒に1番をやってみよう。
Let's try No.1 together.

1分あげるね。
I'll give you 1 minute.

正しい答えは1です。
The correct answer is 1.

問題2番から15番をやってみよう。
Try question No.2 to 15.

10分あげるね。
I'll give you 10 minutes.

答えを確認しましょう、そして説明するね。
Let's check your answers and let me explain.

セクション2には、5問あるよ。
In section 2, there are 5 questions.

問題16番を見て。
Look at question No.16.

2人の会話だよ。

This is a conversation between two people.

誰が話しているか、わかる？

Do you know who is talking?

2人目は何と答えたかな？

What did the second person answer?

選択肢は4つあるよ。

There are four choices.

正しいと思う選択肢を選んでね。

Choose the best choice you think it is correct.

10秒あげるね。

I'll give you 10 seconds.

一緒に問題16番を確認しよう。

Let's check question No.16 together.

正しいと思う選択肢を選んでね。

Choose the best choice you think it is correct.

1分あげるね。

I'll give you 1 minute.

正しい答えは4です。

The correct answer is 4.

わかるかな？

Do you understand?

問題 17 番から 20 番をやってみて。

Try question No.17 to 20.

4 分あげるね。

I'll give you 4 minutes.

答えを確認しましょう。

Let's check your answers.

セクション 3 には、5 問あるよ。

In section 3, there are 5 questions.

21 番を読んでね。

Read No.21.

まず、しっかりと日本語の文を読んでね。

First, read the Japanese sentence carefully.

ホワイトボードを見てね。

Look at the whiteboard.

5 つの単語があるね。

There are five words.

そして 5 つの単語を見て。

And look at five words.

これらの単語をそれぞれの□に入れてみて。

Put these words into each box.

1 分あげるね。

I'll give you 1 minute.

誰かやってくれる人？
Any volunteers?

答えを確認させて。
Let me check your answer.

それが正しいです。
That's correct.

よくできました！
Good job!

では、2番目の□と4番目の□を見て。
Now, look at the second box and the fourth box.

2番目の□は②、4番目の□は⑤です。
The second box is ②, and the fourth box is ⑤.

4つの選択肢を見て。
Look at the four choices.

そう。3だね。
Yes. That's 3.

問題22番から25番をやってみよう。
Try question No.22 to 25.

4分あげるね。
I'll give you 4 minutes.

答えを確認しましょう。
Let's check your answers.

4-A のセクションでは、英文を読まなければなりません。

In section 4-A, you have to read the English sentences.

まず、お知らせのタイトルを読んでね。

First, read the title of the note.

次に、質問を確認して。

Next, check the questions.

2つ質問があるね。

There are two questions.

お知らせの中から答えを見つけてね。

Find the answer from the note.

4-B のセクションでは、メールを読まなければなりません。

In section 4-B, you have to read the e-mails.

メールが2つあるね。

There are two e-mails.

1つ目を見てね。

Look at the first one.

件名を見てね。

Look at the subject.

誰がこのメールを書いたのかな？

Who wrote this e-mail?

2つ目のメールを見て。

Look at the second e-mail.

これは返信だよ。

This is a response e-mail.

3つ質問があるよ。

There are three questions.

メールの中から答えを見つけてね。

Find the answers from e-mails.

4-C のセクションでは、英文を読まなければなりません。

In section 4-C, you have to read the English sentences.

まず、タイトルを読んでね。

First, read the title.

次に、文章の下の注記を見てね。

Next, look at the notation below the paragraphs.

3番目に、質問を確認しましょう。

Third, check the questions.

5つ質問があるね。

There are five questions.

文の中から答えを見つけてね。

Find the answer from the sentences.

これでリーディングのセクションは終わりです。

This is the end of the reading section.

リスニング

リスニングのセクション1には、10問あります。

In listening section 1, there are 10 questions.

10枚の絵があるね。

There are ten pictures.

まず、1番を見て。

First, look at No.1.

CDを聞いて。

Listen to the CD.

2回聞けるよ。

You can listen to it twice.

何番を選んだ？

What number did you choose?

2番が正しい答えだよ。

No.2 is the correct answer.

説明させて。

Let me explain.

では、問題2番から10番をやってみよう。

Now, try question No.2 to 10.

〔10番が終わった後〕
赤ペンか赤エンピツを持っている？

Do you have a red pen or red pencil?

答えを確認しましょう。

Let's check your answers.

セクション2には、10問あるよ。

In section 2, there are 10 questions.

このセクションに、絵はないよ。

In this section, there are no pictures.

選択肢を読まなければなりません。

You have to read the choices.

それらを声に出して読んで。

Read them out loud.

まず、11番を見て。

First, look at No.11.

それらを声に出して読んで。

Read them out loud.

選択肢1を読んで。

Read the choice 1.

選択肢2を読んで。

Read the choice 2.

選択肢3を読んで。

Read the choice 3.

選択肢4を読んで。

Read the choice 4.

では、CDを聞いて。

Now, listen to the CD.

何番を選んだ？

What number did you choose?

2番が正解だよ。

No.2 is the correct answer.

説明させてね。

Let me explain.

次の問題に進みましょう。

Let's move on to the next questions.

問題12番から20番をやってみよう。

Try question No.12 to 20.

答えを確認しましょう。

Let's check your answers.

セクション3には、10問あるよ。

In section 3, there are 10 questions.

まず、21番を見て。

First, look at No.21.

選択肢を読まなければなりません。

You have to read the choices.

それらを声に出して読んで。

Read them out loud.

選択肢1を読んで。

Read the choice 1.

選択肢2を読んで。

Read the choice 2.

選択肢3を読んで。
Read the choice 3.

選択肢4を読んで。
Read the choice 4.

では、CDを聞いて。
Now, listen to the CD.

何番を選んだ？
What number did you choose?

3番が正解だよ。
No.3 is the correct answer.

説明させてね。
Let me explain.

次の問題に進みましょう。
Let's move on to the next questions.

問題22番から30番をやってみよう。
Try question No.22 to 30.

答えを確認しましょう。
Let's check your answers.

これでテストは終わりです。
This is the end of the test.

●著者紹介●

ウィップル道子

兵庫県西脇市出身。関西の大学で学び、その後アメリカ合衆国ユタ州に留学。卒業後、ソルトレイク市の企業に勤務。2000年に日本に帰国後、アメリカ人の夫と英語教室を開校。アルク認定Kiddy CAT英語教室の英語講師を務める。小学校の英語活動、企業の英語研修、通訳、翻訳などに携わる。2012年より英語講師の他に、ESAC認定プロフェッショナル英語学習アドバイザーとして生徒の英語学習管理やアドバイスを開始。2016年よりDMM英会話なんてuKnow?アンカー活動に携わる。J-Shine（NPO法人小学校英語指導者認定協議会）認定の小学校英語指導者資格取得。

アダム・ウィップル

アメリカ合衆国カリフォルニア州出身。ユタ州のカレッジでコミュニケーションを学び、ソルトレイク市の企業に勤務。2000年に来日し、英語教室を開校。アルク認定Kiddy CAT英語教室の英語講師を務める。2001年より兵庫県の公立小学校の英語活動、企業の英語研修、翻訳に携わる。2016年よりDMM英会話なんてuKnow?アンカー活動に携わる。

本書の内容に関するお問い合わせは弊社HPからお願いいたします。

音声DL付き 小学校の英語授業フレーズ3000

2021年 4月 26日 初版発行	著 者	ウィップル道子 アダム・ウィップル
	発行者	石 野 栄 一

明日香出版社

〒112-0005 東京都文京区水道2-11-5
電話 (03) 5395-7650（代 表）
(03) 5395-7654（FAX）
郵便振替 00150-6-183481
https://www.asuka-g.co.jp

■スタッフ■ BP事業部 久松圭祐／藤田知子／藤本さやか／田中裕也／朝倉優梨奈／竹中初音
BS事業部 渡辺久夫／奥本達哉／横尾一樹／関山美保子

印刷 株式会社フクイン
製本 根本製本株式会社
ISBN978-4-7569-2144-4 C0082

本書のコピー、スキャン、デジタル化等の無断複製は著作権法上で禁じられています。
乱丁本・落丁本はお取り替え致します。
©Michiko Whipple, Adam Whipple 2021 Printed in Japan
編集担当 石塚幸子

365 日の日常英会話フレーズブック

長尾和夫　アンディ・バーガー

1月1日から12月31日まで1年間の日常生活を通して、身近な英語表現を学べます。1日1ページずつ、「ダイアローグ」「今日のフレーズ」「Words&Phrases」を学習しながら、ネイティブがよく使う会話表現が身につきます。音声ダウンロード付き。

本体価格 1900 円＋税　B6 並製〈408 ページ〉2020/12 発行　978-4-7569-2124-6

 **英語が話せる！聞こえる！
音をまねするトレーニング**

川本佐奈恵

384 のセンテンスを「音まね」して会話のトレーニングができます。1日5分、まずは 3 ヶ月間、練習しましょう。「文字で読んだら簡単なのに、話せない」状況から抜け出し、「話す・聞く」に自信がつきます。

本体価格 1600 円＋税　B6 変型〈236 ページ〉2015/12 発行　978-4-7569-1810-9

 イギリス英語フレーズブック

ジュミック今井

イギリスへ旅行したり、留学・転勤などでイギリスで生活する人たちが日常の様々なシーンで使える会話表現集。色々な場で使える会話フレーズ（2900）を場面別・状況別に収録。CD 3 枚付き（日本語→英語収録）

本体価格 2700 円＋税　B6 変型〈392 ページ〉2018/01 発行　978-4-7569-1948-9